GOD AND ME AND SOMETIMES IN BETWEEN

Readings To Help You
Stay Close To God

~

TOMBO
Mr Thomas Baumgart

ISBN: 1492156027
ISBN 13: 9781492156024
Library of Congress Control Number: 2013915926
CreateSpace Independent Publishing Platform
North Charleston, South Carolina

Dedication

Thanks to Jeanne and Paul, who have provided wonderful guidance and editing. Thanks also to family and friends who were terrific examples and mentors to me in the creation of this book. Thanks to Sr. Antoinette who gifted me with the nickname Tombo and always reminded me of my many gifts and talents. This book is dedicated to our gracious and generous Lord, the source of life and all good gifts and blessings.

Tombo

God and Me and Sometimes In Between

God provides us with many blessings: from sunrises to sunsets, from parents to siblings, from extended family to friends, from small and intimate celebrations to gigantic weddings and anniversaries. These and many other events in our life are all reminders that God loves us, created us in his image, and wishes us to have life and live that life abundantly.

Sometimes we are very in tune with the Divine. During these times we are confident in where we are going, our relationships are life-giving and nurturing, and our life's path seems orderly and complete. At other times we are in complete disarray because of a death in our family, our career, or our vision. We are extremely confused and in need of healing and direction. And still at other times we seem to be on an even keel in many areas but are a little unsure of ourselves in other facets of our life. Life is fine, but a little fuzzy around the edges. These in between times are times when we need to seek renewal and a better and more complete connection with our God. We need a little direction, encouragement, or comfort.

As you read these pages, those in between times can be mitigated; the edges of our life can become clearer, and our vision of God and his role in our life can become less fuzzy. These readings may help in your eagerness to have God direct your life more closely and be an aid in getting in sync with God's plan.

As humans we constantly need to be reminded of God and his active part in our lives. He is with us always, always gives us his love unconditionally, and constantly provides us with the means to abundant life. When those in between times come, seek God's love and assurance in prayer. Read these pages and allow God's message of love to help you overcome insecurity, loneliness, and doubt, thereby erasing any fuzziness and in-betweeness in your relationship with your God.

Table of Contents

Section One:
U. R. Unique

You are unique. You are a marvelous creation. You are a one-of-a-kind-jewel. There is no one, past or present, who is exactly like you with the same likes, dislikes, feelings, or opinions. God made you to be like no one else. Enjoy and share your God-given gifts and talents with all those people you meet now and in the future.

We have different gifts, according to the grace given us. If a man's gift is prophesying, let him use it in proportion to his faith. If it is serving, let him serve; if it is teaching, let him teach; if it is encouraging, let him encourage; if it is contributing to the needs of others, let him give generously; if it is leadership, let him govern diligently; if it is showing mercy, let him do it cheerfully. Love must be sincere. Hate what is evil; cling to what is good. Be devoted to one another in brotherly love. Honor one another above yourselves. Never be lacking in zeal, but keep your spiritual fervor, serving the Lord. Be joyful in hope, patient in affliction, faithful in prayer. Share with God's people who are in need. Practice hospitality. Bless those who persecute you; bless and do not curse. Rejoice with those who rejoice; mourn with those who mourn. Live in harmony with one another. Do not be proud, but be willing to associate with people of low position. Do not be conceited. Do not repay anyone evil for evil. Be careful to do what is right in the eyes of everybody. If it is possible, as far as it depends on you, live at peace with everyone. Romans 12:6–1

Always Remember you are Unique, Just Like Everybody Else

This comment is meant to be funny. We shouldn't take ourselves so seriously because there are many other people just like us with the same problems and difficulties.

I think the statement makes perfect sense. God has made us unique just like every other human being is one of a kind. He has created each and every person different from everyone else, all five billion of us. That uniqueness includes all those who have come before us and all those who will come after us.

Enjoy your uniqueness. Celebrate your creation. Be appreciative of the other people around you who are also special creations of God.

Dear Lord,
Help me to accept the gifts you have given me. Help me to appreciate the fact that you have created me according to your design. Guide me in the use of those gifts for your honor and glory.

Allow me to accept others as precious gifts too. They are also unique creations of your hand. I pray this through Jesus Christ, our Lord. Amen.

But in fact God has arranged the parts in the body, every one of them, just as he wanted them to be. 1 Corinthians 12:18

Therefore, as we have opportunity, let us do good to all people, especially to those who belong to the family of believers. Galatians 6:10

Everyone who is called by my name, whom I created for my glory, whom I formed and made. The people I formed for myself that they may proclaim my praise. Isaiah 43:7, 21

Just as each of us has one body with many members, and these members do not all have the same function, so in Christ we who are many form one body, and each member belongs to all the others. We have different gifts, according to the grace given us. Romans 12:4–6

Are You Like a Cow or a Pig?

There once were a cow and a pig who resided in the same barn. They often had conversations with each other. Sometimes these conversations became arguments. One nice summer day they had one of these disagreements.

The pig stated that he was more important than the cow. The cow, of course, couldn't agree with that, so she insisted that she was more valuable than the pig.

"Oh, but I am ham for Thanksgiving, and my hooves are used in Jell-O, and I make the neatest wallets," stated the pig proudly. "You, on the other hand, only give milk. I am definitely more valuable in every way compared to you."

The cow couldn't think of any reply, so she meekly agreed with the pig. In her heart she knew she was at least as precious as the pig, but she also wanted the pig to feel important. In the end both animals seemed content—for that day, at least.

We, in our lives, can draw conclusions from the argument between the cow and the pig. It is true that both animals provide products that are useful to humans. But the cow's advantage is that it is constantly giving during its lifetime while the pig is most useful after its death. We are called to be people who are worthwhile while we are alive. We could leave a vast fortune to future generations, but how much more important would it be to be "worth a fortune" while we are alive? Think of all the situations you encounter where you can make the lives of your fellow human beings more worthwhile. Start being productive today while you are still alive.

One man gives freely, yet gains even more; another withholds unduly, but comes to poverty. A generous man will prosper; he who refreshes others will himself be refreshed. Proverbs 11:24, 25

If you spend yourselves in behalf of the hungry and satisfy the needs of the oppressed, then your light will rise in the darkness, and your night will become like the noonday. Isaiah 58:10

The King will reply, "I tell you the truth, whatever you did for one of the least of these brothers of mine, you did for me." Matthew 25:40

I urge you therefore, brothers, by the mercies of God, to offer your bodies as a living sacrifice, holy and pleasing to God, your spiritual worship. Do not conform yourselves to this age but be transformed by the renewal of your mind, that you may discern what is the will of God, what is good and pleasing and perfect. Romans 12:1, 2

Be the Best of Whatever You Are

I can't sing well. I can't play a musical instrument. I can't spike a volleyball. I'm not a homerun hitter.

If you can't be a pine on the top of the hill
Be a scrub in the valley—but be
The best little scrub by the side of the hill;
Be a bush, if you can't be a tree.

I can't sing well, but I certainly can provide substance and support to our church congregation during mass.

If you can't be a bush, be a bit of grass,
And some highway happier make;
If you can't be a muskie, then just be a bass—
But the liveliest bass in the lake!

I can't play a musical instrument, but I do have tapes and CDs that I can use to enliven a Bible study or a prayer service.

We can't all be captains, we've got to be crew,
There's something for all of us here.
There's big work to do and there's lesser to do
And the task we must do is the near.

I can't spike the volleyball over the net, but I can be a setter for someone who can. I can make sure I am always at the game so we don't forfeit because we don't have enough players.

If you can't be a highway, then just be a trail,
If you can't be the sun, be a star;
It isn't by size that you win or you fail—
Be the best of whatever you are!

I'm not a homerun hitter, but I can get on base so I can score when the homerun hitter connects with the next pitch.

This poem by Douglas Malloch reminds me that I shouldn't worry about what I can't do, but rather I should worry about what I can do. If the world was all doctors, where would the patients be? Who would provide nursing care when the doctor was not there? Who would wash the sheets, make the beds, and clean the floors? Clearly many skills from many people are needed to make a successful clinic or hospital experience.

What I need to concentrate on is how well I am going to be who I am. God has given me unique talents and treasures and wants me to use them and develop them according to his plan. God will judge me on my faith and how well I used that faith to help others. God will provide me with strength, support and knowledge so I can be his hands, feet and compassion to my fellow human being.

If I don't become the best person I can be then some need will go unfulfilled, some problem will not be solved, some sorrow will not be erased, and some joy will not be celebrated. The more I enjoy and develop myself, the more aid and support I can give to others. I need to be my own unique part of the body of Christ and do my part for the success of the rest of the body. With faith in God and support from his church, sacraments, and other Christians, I can be successful in that task.

Just as each of us has one body with many members, and these members do not all have the same function, so in Christ we who are many form one body, and each member belongs to all the others.

We have different gifts, according to the grace given us. If a man's gift is prophesying, let him use it in proportion to his faith. If it is serving, let him serve; if it is teaching, let him teach; if it is encouraging, let him encourage; if it is contributing to the needs of others, let him give generously; if it is leadership, let him govern diligently; if it is showing mercy, let him do it cheerfully. Love must be sincere.

Hate what is evil; cling to what is good. Be devoted to one another in brotherly love. Honor one another above yourselves. Never be lacking in zeal, but keep your spiritual fervor, serving the Lord. Be joyful in hope, patient in affliction, faithful in prayer. Share with God's people who are in need. Practice hospitality.

Bless those who persecute you; bless and do not curse. Rejoice with those who rejoice; mourn with those who mourn. Live in harmony with one another. Do not be proud, but be willing to associate with people of low position. Do not be conceited. Do not repay anyone evil for evil. Be careful to do what is right in the eyes of everybody. If it is possible, as far as it depends on you, live at peace with everyone. Romans 12:4–18

Gifts

Take what you have
   Expand
   Develop
   Enjoy
Share with others
   Today
   Tomorrow
   Always
Give thanks to God
   Now
   Often
   Humbly

The above poem by Tom reminds us that we are given gifts from God and they are meant to be appreciated and share with others as often as possible.

The Lord appeared to us in the past, saying: "I have loved you with an everlasting love; I have drawn you with loving-kindness." Jeremiah 31:3

May our Lord Jesus Christ himself and God our father, who loved us and by his grace gave us eternal encouragement and good hope, encourage your hearts and strengthen you in every good deed and word. 2 Thessalonians 2:16, 17

Is it not to share your food with the hungry and to provide the poor wanderer with shelter—when you see the naked, to clothe him, and not to turn away from your own flesh and blood? Then your light will break forth like the dawn, and your healing will quickly appear; then your righteousness will go before you, and the glory of the Lord will be your rear guard. Isaiah 58:7, 8

Talents

Talents are those wonderful things that we
All have and need to share with others.
Let us remember that God has
Entitled us to these gifts, and we are
Not meant to keep them to ourselves.
Today let us make a pledge to
Share, enjoy, and develop them the best we can.

Gifts and talents are precious abilities given to us by a generous and loving God. They are meant for our unique use but also as blessings to be shared with the many people we interact with in our journey here on earth. The more they are shared the greater effect they will have on our self, our neighbors, community and our world.

I am the true vine, and my father is the vine grower. He takes away every branch in me that does not bear fruit, and everyone that does he prunes so that it bears more fruit. You are already pruned because of the word that I spoke to you. Remain in me, as I remain in you. Just as a branch cannot bear fruit on its own unless it remains on the vine, so neither can you unless you remain in me. I am the vine, you are the branches. Whoever remains in me and I in him will bear much fruit, because without me you can do nothing. Anyone who does not remain in me will be thrown out like a branch and wither; people will gather them and throw them into a fire and they will be burned. If you remain in me and my words remain in you, ask for whatever you want and it will be done for you. By this is my Father glorified, that you bear much fruit and become my disciples. I have told you this so that my joy may be in you and your joy may be complete. This is my commandment: love one another as I love you. John 15:1–8;11–12

God Made You an Original; Don't Die a Copy Thelma Wells

Drink the right drink, and you will be popular. Go to the "in" places to show your class. Meet with the right people everyone will notice you. Wear the latest clothing and be "hip," "hot," "bad," or whatever the latest catchphrase is. It all comes down to being like everyone else, to lose your individuality, to fit in, to mold your thinking to the groups' concepts of what is right and good and proper. It all means a loss of self. You become a clone to everyone else who wants to fit into society's mold. You no longer reflect the unique individual that God created and become less than what you were meant to be.

The mass media is strong and persistent. It creates the norm and encourages people to follow that pattern. People in the communications business want you to think they know what is best for you. They want you to accept their ideas of what is proper, healthful, authentic, and fulfilling. They want you to accept them as knowledgeable and reliable and their message is life-giving and rewarding.

How easy is it to buy the latest SUV because the media tells us we need it? If we own it, we will be leaders. We will blaze our own trails and be pioneers and rugged individuals who lead adventurous lives. We shouldn't consider the wasteful use of gas by the vehicle. Nor should we be concerned that we probably will not use it to climb mountains, or explore canyons, or even watch the sun go down in some remote rocky vista. Most of the time it will be used to go to and from work, carry groceries and children, and be a delivery van for soccer kids. The fantasy of the SUV simply does not match the reality of our lives. But too often we buy into the concept and ignore the facts. These pressures to accept media messages are everywhere.

God, on the other hand, has formed us as individuals. We are not meant to blindly follow the latest trends. We are created to critically analyze the messages society sends our way. If it is helpful to our spiritual life, then we should accept it. If it is harmful, we need to reject the message. That will be a constant battle in our lives: listening to the media and society or to God. The more we are in tune with God, the more of an individual we will become and less like a copy of what society has molded. Pray for God's light and encouragement that we may make life-giving choices rather than decisions that will create clones of what society says we should be. Pray often because the media blitz and society's message is constant, and if we are not careful it will become the "idol" we choose to follow. Choose God instead. Choose life.

I will sprinkle clean water on you, and you will be clean; I will cleanse you from all your impurities and from all your idols. I will give you a new heart and put a new spirit in you; I will remove from you your heart of stone and give you a heart of flesh. Ezekiel 36:25, 26

Junk

In his book *God's Two-Minute Warning*, John Hagee describes going to the junkyard looking for a part. In the presence of the owner, he mentioned the word "junkyard." The owner stated that what he was looking for was not junk because junk had no value to anyone. Instead, he was looking for a part that had a possibility. That possibility made the part something valuable, not junk.

So what in our lives makes us something other than junk? What value are we to other people? No, it doesn't matter how many skills or talents we possess. It all depends on love. Love makes anything and everything valuable. In the Bible we learn that without love we are nothing but a noisy gong. Our knowledge, money, and possessions amount to nothing without love.

Where do we find our pattern for love? Jesus, of course, is the model we need to follow. He taught us how to love. He taught us about forgiveness. He taught us how to be honest, not hypocritical. He instructed us to be compassionate. He told us to be like children. Take time to peruse your Bible. Learn about Jesus and how to be a loving person.

If I speak in the tongues of men and of angels, but have not love, I am only a resounding gong or a clanging cymbal. If I have the gift of prophecy and can fathom all mysteries and all knowledge, and if I have a faith that can move mountains, but have not love, I am nothing. If I give all I possess to the poor and surrender my body to the flames, but have not love, I gain nothing.

Love is patient, love is kind. It does not envy, it does not boast, it is not proud. It is not rude, it is not self-seeking, it is not easily angered, it keeps no record of wrongs. Love does not delight in evil but rejoices with the truth. It always protects, always trusts, always hopes, always perseveres. Love never fails.

But where there are prophecies, they will cease; where there are tongues, they will be stilled; where there is knowledge, it will pass away. For we know in part and we prophesy in part, but when perfection comes, the imperfect disappears.

When I was a child, I talked like a child, I thought like a child, I reasoned like a child. When I became a man, I put childish ways behind me. Now we see but a poor reflection as in a mirror; then we shall see face to face. Now I know in part; then I shall know fully, even as I am fully known. And now these three remain: faith, hope and love. But the greatest of these is love. 1 Corinthians 13:1–13

Keys

Jim, a priest and high school teacher, was approaching school on his first day of class. He noticed a freshman boy all dressed up for his first day of school. The priest approached the boy and asked why he was standing there. The boy replied that he was waiting for someone to open up the school because he was eager to get started. The priest took his keys and began to open the door. The boy exclaimed that he knew the priest was a teacher because he had the keys. That gave the priest the idea that he held the power of unlocking adventures and challenges for students, or he could keep the students locked out of those experiences. It was up to him. That concept of the keys kept him motivated for forty years.

What about us? What keys do we possess? Where can we open up doors or keep them shut in dealing with the people in our lives? Where will we get inspiration and motivation to be door-openers during the boring or difficult times in our lives?

We could start our voyage of discovery by listing all our qualities. We could also get information from people who know us well. That would give us an accurate tally of our talents.

Once we have looked at our abilities, it's time to decide which talents we have been using to open up doors to our self and others and which ones we have used to hinder that process. Next we need to plan on how to do a better job both in the areas in which we are doing well and in the areas where we could use improvement. Which strategies will we use to begin our change?

Once we have the information and strategies organized, we need to seek God's help. His grace and guidance is necessary for any major change in our attitudes and habits. We should pray many times for God's inspiration. Then we need to wait. During the time of waiting, we should be continually praying for God's help to see if our plans need modification. When we feel comfortable we can begin the task of changing ourselves.

God has promised to be with us, to guide us, to support us in his plan for our lives. We have confidence He will keep his word and enable us to be those keys that open people up to their potential and encourage them to grow and change, to become the best possible. Every time you put your keys into your car, may that be a reminder to you of the valuable key that you are to yourself and someone else.

Let us then approach the throne of grace with confidence, so that we may receive mercy and find grace to help us in our time of need. Hebrews 4:16

Those who are wise will shine like the brightness of the heavens, and those who lead many to righteousness, like the stars for ever and ever. Daniel 12:3

I tell you the truth, anyone who has faith in me will do what I have been doing. He will do even greater things than these, because I am going to the father. John 14:12

A Masterpiece

Did you ever want to own your own masterpiece by Michelangelo, Bernini, or da Vinci? Well, you can. Pick up a Bible— a masterpiece whose words will outlast any painting, sculpture, or monument. You can be "rich" in advice, wisdom, and examples when you read your Bible daily.

Do not let this Book of the Law depart from your mouth; meditate on it day and night, so that you may be careful to do everything written in it. Then you will be prosperous and successful. Joshua 1:8

He has raised up a horn of salvation for us in the house of his servant David (as he said through his holy prophets of long ago), "Praise be to the Lord, the God of Israel, because he has come and has redeemed his people. to shine on those living in darkness and in the shadow of death, to guide our feet into the path of peace." Luke 1:69, 70, 79

All Scripture is God-breathed and is useful for teaching, rebuking, correcting and training in righteousness, so that the man of God may be thoroughly equipped for every good work. 2 Timothy 3:16, 17

To the Jews who had believed him, Jesus said, "If you hold to my teaching, you are really my disciples. Then you will know the truth, and the truth will set you free." John 8:31, 32

Never Too Late

No one can go back and make a brand new start. Anyone can start from now and make a brand new ending. Loris Ann Greco

Smokers who quit cannot undo all the damage done to their lungs. But they can reduce the problems in the future. Knowing there will be future benefits from not smoking should inspire them to quit the habit. The future can be changed, but the past has to be accepted. When the habit is kicked, so should guilt and regret for our past actions be erased from our memory. Concentration should be on the future and not what has happened yesterday or the day before yesterday.

With God it's possible to start anew. God allows "do-overs" just like kids do in a game. God will love and support the new us with open arms. His strength and guidance is available twenty-four hours a day. There will be no obstacles from receiving support from our Creator. God has an inexhaustible supply of love ready to be given to us as needed. All we need to do is ask.

For I am convinced that neither death nor life, neither angels nor demons, neither the present nor the future, nor any powers, neither height nor depth, nor anything else in all creation, will be able to separate us from the love of God that is in Christ Jesus our Lord. Romans 8:38, 39

Once we ask for help, change can occur. That change will affect the outcome of our life. Our past will no longer be relevant to our future. Only our present effort will be counted.

So do not fear, for I am with you; do not be dismayed, for I am your God. I will strengthen you and help you; I will uphold you with my righteous right hand. Isaiah 41:10

Therefore, if anyone is in Christ, he is a new creation; the old has gone, the new has come! 2 Corinthians 5:17

Start today by forgetting the past. Focus on adjusting your future seeking God's help to make that alteration. Pray, read scripture, seek assistance from friends, and begin work on changing your ancient outdated and useless habits and replacing them with fresh, new, beneficial habits. It's never too late!

U

You are unique, one of a kind, a marvelous creation from an awesome God. He does not create junk, so you must be important. There is no one, past or present, who is exactly like you, with your unique gifts and talents. You are a jewel, a priceless gem, something worth a great deal.

Should U feel less than spectacular? NO!
Should U feel like you don't measure up? NO!
Should U feel that you have no impact on other people's lives? NO!
Should U feel that you are in any way less worthy to be a child of God? NO!

U should feel like you are a member of God's family.
U should feel that your efforts are valuable.
U should feel grateful for the specific gifts and talents that you alone have.
U should feel that you have a God-given role to play in this vast universe.

Take time to evaluate your talents (from your point of view and from the view of someone else who knows you). Thank God for those gifts. Then pray that he will help you to grow and change into a more perfect you. He will help, of course, but it is nice to ask for assistance and guidance. Once you have done that, make a commitment to improve in *one* area of your life. God's word, his church, and his sacraments will help you in your growth. Once you have made progress in one area, start on another. Over time you will see a much different person in the mirror than the one you saw before this process. You won't see day-to-day change, but you'll see appreciable growth only after a period of time. Then you will realize that you have matured in your faith and your abilities. You will have improved in one or more areas of your life causing others to notice the differences in you. Having had some success in one area, you will be eager to improve in other segments of your life. This continued growth will happen with the aid of God until you are ready to leave this earthly life.

Trees change. Caterpillars change. Flowers change. People change, and so will you. Enjoy the journey. Remember God is with you every step of the way, and with God all things are possible, even a more perfect U.

I will lead the blind by ways they have not known, along unfamiliar paths I will guide them; I will turn the darkness into light before them and make the rough places smooth. These are the things I will do; I will not forsake them. Isaiah 42:16

For this very reason, make every effort to add to your faith goodness; and to goodness, knowledge; and to knowledge, self-control; and to self-control, perseverance; and to perseverance, godliness; and to godliness, brotherly kindness; and to brotherly kindness, love. 2 Peter 1:5–7

You are Nothing but a Lemon!

How often do we think we are like a lemon? Sometimes we feel that we are all alike—there isn't much difference between myself and anyone else. How do we stand out? Or we might think that we have so many flaws and imperfections that we can't be worth much. Lemons don't taste very sweet.

The "pity pot" mentality doesn't serve us well. It also doesn't help us to realize how wonderful and gracious our God is. We need to be reoriented.

God does love us like a lemon. Even though we look pretty much the same, we are all quite different. As we look at lemons we see ridges, valleys, different shading and hues, and a variety of lengths and widths. God know us, imperfections and all. He created us to be unique and can pick us out of any crowd at any time. We are not strangers to God.

When sugar is added to lemon juice, it becomes a cool, refreshing, and tasty drink. That is what God does for us. He adds the sugar to make us cool, life-giving, and interesting. With him we are meant to grow and develop into something wonderful. The choice is ours. We can allow God to renew, energize, and change us, or we can think of ourselves as poor, undesirable, and tart lemons. What will our choice be? Will we be celebrating our uniqueness or bemoaning our sameness?

"Consider how the lilies grow. They do not labor or spin. Yet I tell you, not even Solomon in all his splendor was dressed like one of these. If that is how God clothes the grass of the field, which is here today, and tomorrow is thrown into the fire, how much more will he clothe you, O you of little faith! And do not set your heart on what you will eat or drink; do not worry about it. For the pagan world runs after all such things, and your Father knows that you need them. But seek his kingdom, and these things will be given to you as well. Do not be afraid, little flock, for your Father has been pleased to give you the kingdom." Luke 12:22–32

You are Unique

In all the world there is no one who is exactly like you.

No one has your smile.
No one has your sense of humor.
Your way of looking at things is unique.
No one has exactly your strengths and weaknesses.
No one relates to others, confides in others like you.
Your thoughts and cares are original.
Your insights into life are like no one else's.
Your many good traits are yours alone.
The gifts and talents you have are special.
You have no replacement in the entire universe.
Your distinctive behaviors cannot be matched.

Enjoy your uniqueness. Be satisfied that you are like no one else. Be content with your weaknesses, but be willing to grow and change. Be what only you can be. Compare yourself with no one. You are not superior to anyone else or less desirable, just different and unique.

For you created my inmost being; you knit me together in my mother's womb. I praise you because I am fearfully and wonderfully made; your works are wonderful, I know full well. Psalm 139:13, 14

The Lord appeared to us in the past, saying; "I have loved you with an everlasting love; I have drawn you with loving-kindness." Jeremiah 31:3

Celebrate your uniqueness!

Section Two:
God's Love for Us

God loves us with an everlasting love. He created us in his own image and sent his son to die for us and our transgressions. When it comes to love, God is the Alpha and Omega, the beginning and end and everything in between. We need to accept God's gracious love, internalize it, and then share that love with the people we meet.

The Lord appeared to us in the past, saying: "I have loved you with an everlasting love; I have drawn you with loving-kindness. Jeremiah 31:3

For God so loved the world that he gave his one and only son, that whoever believes in him shall not perish but have eternal life. John 3:16

But because of his great love for us, God, who is rich in mercy, made us alive with Christ even when we were dead in transgressions—it is by grace you have been saved. And God raised us up with Christ and seated us with him in the heavenly realms in Christ Jesus, in order that in the coming ages he might show the incomparable riches of his grace, expressed in his kindness to us in Christ Jesus. Ephesians 2:4–7

Amazing Grace

Amazing grace! How sweet the sound that saved a wretch like me!

This is good and pleasing to God our savior, who wills everyone to be saved and to come to knowledge of the truth. For there is one God. There is also one mediator between God and the human race, Christ Jesus, himself human, who gave himself as ransom for all. This was the testimony at the proper time. 1 Timothy 2:3–6

So we are ambassadors for Christ, as if God were appealing through us. We implore you on behalf of Christ, be reconciled to God. For our sake he made him to be sin who did not know sin, so that we might become the righteousness of God in him. 2 Corinthians 5:21, 22

I once was lost, but now am found; was blind but now I see.

But when the kindness and generous love of God our savior appeared, not because of any righteous deeds we had done but because of his mercy, he saved us through the bath of rebirth and renewal by the Holy Spirit, whom he richly poured out on us through Jesus Christ our savior. Titus 3:4–6

Everything indeed is for you, so that the grace bestowed in abundance on more and more people may cause the thanksgiving to overflow for the glory of God. 2 Corinthians 4:15

Grace has come to us freely and abundantly. What will we do in return? Do we thank God daily for his marvelous blessings? Do we use his gifts to us to help others? Do we see the God given talents in others?

Take a moment to appreciate and praise God today spending some special time with him in prayer. Dedicate your work and efforts of the day to his honor and glory and continue to use his grace to grow spiritually.

Therefore, beloved, since you are forewarned, be on your guard not to be led into the error of the unprincipled and to fall from your own stability. But grow in grace and in the knowledge of our Lord and savior Jesus Christ. To him be glory now and to the day of eternity. (Amen.) 2 Peter 3:17, 18

The Lord has promised good to me, his word my hope secures. He will my shield and portion be as long as life endures. John Newton

A Most Precious Possession

A young convert approached a pastor with a question. "How can the holy God forgive a sinner? Isn't God repulsed with all the hatred and jealousy that fills people?"

The pastor looked warmly at his young, enthusiastic friend and said, "You are the third generation in a family of master furniture makers. Tell me, if a fine table that your grandfather made was scratched, would you throw it away?"

"Of course not," the young man exclaimed. "A scratch can hardly alter the character of a fine piece of furniture."

"And," the pastor continued, "if you nicked a well-crafted oak rocker, would you toss it away?"

"Throw it away?" the young man exclaimed. "Even with a few scratches, quality furniture is sturdy and valuable."

"You have spoken like a true craftsman," the pastor replied. "You share that spirit with our creator God who continues to find his human creation precious and valuable in spite of their obvious flaws."

Taken from *Stories for the Journey* *by* William R. White

Whenever we feel incapable, not smart enough or not up to the task at hand, remember we are not the master craftsman, God is. He will use our imperfection and shortcomings to accomplish his will. We need to have faith that our God can do what he says he is capable of doing. We do our best and leave the rest up to God.

"My grace is sufficient for you, for power is made perfect in weakness." I will rather boast most gladly of my weaknesses, in order that the power of Christ may dwell with me. Therefore, I am content with weaknesses, insults, hardships, persecutions, and constraints, for the sake of Christ, for when I am weak, then I am strong. 2 Corinthians 12:9, 10

Armed With Faith

Are you armed with faith? The Lord provides us with faith. He will nourish and develop that faith. He will do that through his word and sacraments. The more you read scripture and receive the sacraments, the better able you will be to meet the challenges of evil brought to us by the devil and his associates. If the devil is like a lion who is ready to devour us as stated in 1 Peter 5:8, 9, then we need to be prepared. Without a strong faith we don't stand a chance to overcome the power of the evil one. Our Lord lovingly gives us all the protections we need to overcome evil in all its forms.

Put on the armor of God so that you may be able to stand firm against the tactics of the devil. For our struggle is not with flesh and blood but with the principalities, with the powers, with the world rulers of this present darkness, with the evil spirits in the heavens. Therefore, put on the armor of God, that you may be able to resist on the evil day and, having done everything, to hold your ground. So stand fast with your loins girded in truth, clothed with righteousness as a breastplate, and your feet shod in readiness for the gospel of peace. In all circumstances, hold faith as a shield, to quench all (the) flaming arrows of the evil one. And take the helmet of salvation and the sword of the Spirit, which is the word of God. Ephesians 6:11–17

We cannot be "wishy washy" in our faith, but rather we need to be completely committed to God and his commands. We must be armed and dangerous when dealing with the devil. If we do that, no temptation will be too great for us to overcome.

Amen, I say to you, if you have faith the size of a mustard seed, you will say to this mountain, "Move from here to there," and it will move. Nothing will be impossible for you. Matthew 17:20

The best time to be prepared for battle is before the confrontation begins. Start your day with prayer, put on the armor of God as written in Ephesians 6:13–17, and relax in the knowledge that God will provide you with whatever you need.

So submit yourselves to God. Resist the devil, and he will flee from you. James 4:7 You believe that God is one. You do well. Even the demons believe that and tremble. James 2:19

Start your day armed with faith and you will end your day knowing you were successful in following God's will and defeating the temptations of the devil.

Birth/Death/Rebirth

Married/Single/Extended Family
Birth/Death/Resurrection
Teach/Retire/Volunteer
Child/Adult/Grandchildren
Summer/Winter/Spring
Job/Fired or Downsized/New Job

Throughout my life I will experience many difficulties and changes in my life style (deaths) like the ones above that can easily cause me to become despondent. I can dwell on my problems and feel sorry for myself, or I can remember that because of God's grace I have the ability to rise from the ashes. Where there is death and destruction, God will sustain me.

God is our refuge and our strength, an ever-present help in distress. Thus we do not fear, though earth be shaken and mountains quake to the depths of the sea. Psalm 46:1–3

When challenges come to me, my God will provide strength through his word, his sacraments and his children. Thus, God will bolster me to overcome the challenges I face.

You who fear the Lord, give praise! All descendants of Jacob, give honor; show reverence, all descendants of Israel! For God has not spurned or disdained the misery of this poor wretch, did not turn away from me, but heard me when I cried out. Psalm 22:24, 25

When I am mired in my problems, God's graces will provide me with knowledge and fortitude. I am never alone in tackling the problems in my life.

Though I walk in the midst of dangers, you guard my life when my enemies rage. You stretch out your hand; your right hand saves me. The Lord is with me to the end. Lord, your love endures forever. Never forsake the work of your hands! Psalm 138:7, 8

Wait for the Lord, take courage; be stouthearted, wait for the Lord! Psalm 27:14

Where there is death God provides life. His help is only a prayer away, so nothing in my life need worry me.

Come to me, all you who labor and are burdened, and I will give you rest. Take my yoke upon you and learn from me, for I am meek and humble of heart; and you will find rest for your selves. For my yoke is easy, and my burden light. Matthew 11:28–30

For as Christ's sufferings overflow to us, so through Christ does our encouragement also overflow. 2 Corinthians 1:5

With God's help I will have a rebirth many times in my life. Whatever challenges come my way I know that God will see me through them and will help me to flourish once again. Just as Christ rose from the dead, I will rise from the difficulties in my life.

But when the kindness and generous love of God our savior appeared, not because of any righteous deeds we had done but because of his mercy, he saved us through the bath of rebirth and renewal by the holy Spirit, whom he richly poured out on us through Jesus Christ our savior, so that we might be justified by his grace and become heirs in hope of eternal life. Titus 3:4–6

A thief comes only to steal and slaughter and destroy; I came so that they might have life and have it more abundantly. John 10:10

I will praise my God for his great love, power, and mercy and eagerly look forward to reigning with him in heaven when my earthly life is done.

Blessed be the God and Father of our Lord Jesus Christ, who in his great mercy gave us a new birth to a living hope through the resurrection of Jesus Christ from the dead, to an inheritance that is imperishable, undefiled, and unfading, kept in heaven for you who by the power of God are safeguarded through faith, to a salvation that is ready to be revealed in the final time. 1 Peter 1:3–5

Blessings From Above

Find your delight in the Lord who will give you your heart's desire. Psalm 37:4

For he satisfied the thirsty, filled the hungry with good things. Psalm 107:9

Did you thank the Lord for your bonus at work? Were you grateful when you won the prize you wanted at the raffle? Did you give thanks when you received money you didn't expect?

A thief comes only to steal and slaughter and destroy; I came so that they might have life and have it more abundantly. John 10:10

But now I am coming to you. I speak this in the world so that they may share my joy completely. John 17:13

Have you given praise and thanksgiving to God for your excellent choice in picking a house? A different job? A new city to live in? Have you been grateful for the minor and the significant happenings in your life that left a smile on your face?

For the wages of sin is death, but the gift of God is eternal life in Christ Jesus our Lord. Romans 6:23

If you then, who are wicked, know how to give good gifts to your children, how much more will the Father in heaven give the Holy Spirit to those who ask him? Luke 11:13

Have you made it a point to invite the Lord to the many joyous events in your life, such as: a wedding, a baby shower, a promotion, a new house, a birthday, or a recovery from illness?

Blessed is the person who trusts in the Lord, whose hope is the Lord. Jeremiah 17:7

If we trust in the Lord then why don't we include him in everything in our life from the very ordinary to the extraordinary? Start anew by inviting the Creator of the universe to be a part of everything in your life. The Lord is anxiously waiting for your invitation.

41

Bread and Life

Man cannot live by bread alone; he needs peanut butter. Barbara Johnson

Life. Enjoy! Celebrate! Shout with joy! Yes, God has meant for us to live life and live it abundantly. He will provide the peanut butter on our bread. So don't worry. Be happy. Celebrate!

I will bless her with abundant provisions; her poor will I satisfy with food. Psalm 132:15

You will have plenty to eat, until you are full, and you will praise the name of the Lord your God, who has worked wonders for you; never again will my people be shamed. Joel 2:26

He grants peace to your borders and satisfies you with the finest of wheat. Psalm 147:14

So do not worry, saying, "What shall we eat?" or "What shall we drink?" or "What shall we wear?" For the pagans run after all these things, and your heavenly Father "knows that you need them. But seek first his kingdom and his righteousness, and all these things will be given to you as well. Matthew 6:31–33

Children

When Jesus saw this, he was indignant. He said to them, "Let the little children come to me, and do not hinder them, for the kingdom of God belongs to such as these. I tell you the truth, anyone who will not receive the kingdom of God like a little child will never enter it." And he took the children in his arms, put his hands on them and blessed them. Mark 10:14–16

How can you be more like a child? How will you recapture that sense of awe? Will you redevelop your sense of trust? Can you nurture an aura of excitement? Do you have complete faith? Is life seen as an adventure full of possibilities? Can you accept others without prejudice?

These and many other questions may help you develop the child-like relationship you need with God. Take time to ponder these questions and decide how you can adapt them and others to fit snugly into your new life.

Clouds

Whenever clouds appear in our life God is there. If they seem dark and threatening God is there. If they are white and billowy and full of promise God is there. No matter the size, shape or intensity of the clouds God is by our side holding our hand and guiding our steps.

Wow! The wedding went wonderfully! The arrangements went on without a hitch. The bride looked radiant and the groom had a huge smile splattered over his face. All the in-laws were cheerful and mingled with each other with great excitement. The little kids were cute and well-behaved. Nothing was out of place. God couldn't be happier with the way the wedding unfolded.

Boy, it is tough to lose a child so young. The parents are devastated. The brothers and sisters are in a daze. The entire town showed up for the church service and funeral to express their sorrow. There was a somber tone throughout the area. God grieved for the survivors.

We need to remember that God is our constant companion whether we are on top of the world or in the garbage heap and anything that happens to us in between those two extremes. God is available to encourage, strengthen, cajole, forgive and celebrate. What ever happens in our lives God is there. He never takes a vacation, calls in sick or simply forgets when it comes to being with us. We couldn't ask for a more loyal or dedicated friend.

God works through his church and sacraments, our friends, relatives, and coworkers, and a whole hosts of events in our lives to provide the support we need. God's abilities and resources are endless. When it comes to our needs, "too tired to help" are words that never come from the lips of God. He is always ready and eager to come to our aid. So the next time you are walking on clouds, or stuck under them, remember that God is there to hold your hand and steer you in the right direction in order navigate the different clouds in our lives.

But you do see; you do observe this misery and sorrow; you take the matter in hand. To you the helpless can entrust their cause; you are the defender of orphans. Psalm 10:14

The Lord is my strength and my shield, in whom my heart trusted and found help. So my heart rejoices; with my song I praise my God. Psalm 28:7

For seven days you shall celebrate this pilgrim feast in honor of the Lord, your God, in the place which he chooses; since the Lord, your God, has blessed you in all your crops and in all your undertakings, you shall do naught but make merry. Deuteronomy 16:15

Until now you have not asked anything in my name; ask and you will receive, so that your joy may be complete. John 16:24

CPR

We all know what CPR stands for. If you are a coffee drinker it might mean Coffee Provides Resuscitation. That idea should get us thinking, "What provides us with the means to meet the rigors of the day?"

For some people, coffee is the necessary ingredient they need to help them jump start the day. To some people, it might be a morning jog or a trip to the gym. For still others it might be a long hot shower that gets their blood pumping. It could also be some soothing or relaxing music. A better start than all of these methods should be beginning our day with God.

Yes, God's word in written or oral form could be the perfect way for us to prepare for our day. His inspiration can be found in Holy Scripture, meditations, and numerous types of booklets. Who better to begin our day than the Creator of the world? Who better to rely on than the King of Kings? Who better to build our understanding of ourselves and our world than the author of the Bible, the greatest selling book of all time? God is more efficient and essential than coffee or any other stimulant because he can last us a whole lifetime, not just until the caffeine wears off or our "runner's high" becomes just a pleasant memory.

God is ready, willing, and able to be the great stimulus in our life. All we need to do is seek him out and let him provide for our needs. It doesn't take a long, cold trip to Starbucks or Gold's Gym or sitting in the shower waiting for the water to be just the right temperature. God is close by, only a prayer away. He is available, night and day, in the Bible. He even provides "perks" for us in the form of his church, sacraments, and people. God gives us the "oomph" we need because he loves us dearly and will do anything so we can enjoy and share eternal life with him.

Get your resuscitation today and tomorrow and every day from God's word. Don't rely on coffee or exercise or any other temporary stimulant.

Draw near to God, and he will draw near to you. Humble yourselves before the Lord and he will exalt you. James 4:8

Indeed, the word of God is living and effective, sharper than any two-edged sword, penetrating even between soul and spirit, joints and marrow, and able to discern reflections and thoughts of the heart. Hebrews 4:12

Thus faith comes from what is heard, and what is heard comes through the word of Christ. Romans 10:17

Like newborn infants, long for pure spiritual milk so that through it you may grow into salvation, for you have tasted that the Lord is good. 1 Peter 2:2, 3

Difficult Times

May the following short phrases help you to remember when difficult times enter your lives God is already there to soothe, encourage and restore your mind and spirit.

When I am feeble my God is strong and courageous.

When I forget to be happy Jesus remembers what is important.

When I am lonely the Holy Spirit comforts me.

God's words help me to open up when I pull inside myself.

Jesus provides me with insight in times I am unsure or baffled.

The Holy Spirit says I can in those time I am sure I can't.

Whether it be troubles, heartache or loneliness I look to my God for aid, release or friendship.

Peace I leave with you; my peace I give to you. Not as the world gives do I give to you. Do not let your hearts be troubled or afraid. John 14:27

Behold, the hour is coming and has arrived when each of you will be scattered to his own home and you will leave me alone. But I am not alone, because the Father is with me. I have told you this so that you might have peace in me. In the world you will have trouble, but take courage, I have conquered the world." John 16:32–33

Finally, brothers, rejoice. Mend your ways, encourage one another, agree with one another, live in peace, and the God of love and peace will be with you. 2 Corinthians 13:11–13

The concern of the flesh is death, but the concern of the spirit is life and peace. For the concern of the flesh is hostility toward God; it does not submit to God, nor can it, and those who are in flesh cannot please God. But you are not in the flesh; on the contrary, you are in the spirit, if only the Spirit of God dwells in you. Whoever does not have the Spirit of Christ does not belong to him. But if Christ is in you, although the body is dead because of sin, the spirit is alive because the one who raised Christ from the dead will give life to your mortal bodies also, through his Spirit that dwells in you. Consequently, brothers, we are not debtors to the flesh, to live according to the flesh. For if you live according to the flesh, you will die, but if by the spirit you put to death the deeds of the body, you will live. Romans 8:6–13

Rejoice in the Lord always. I shall say it again: rejoice. Your kindness should be known to all. The Lord is near. Have no anxiety at all, but in everything, by prayer and petition, with thanksgiving, make your request known to God. Then the peace of God that surpasses all understanding will guard your hearts and minds in Christ Jesus. Philippians 4:4–7

Five Dollars' Worth

Father Mark started his homily by asking the children of Saint Elizabeth Ann Seton Church if they would like what he was holding in his hand. All the hands of the children were raised because they would like the five-dollar bill. Father Mark then proceeded to crumble up the bill and then asked again if the children wanted the money. The response was unanimous: yes. The question was asked again after Father Mark had pretended to spit on the money. Still the children were eager to have the cash. The last example Father Mark gave was to stomp on the bill. Without fail the "little people" wanted the money. He explained how we were like the five-dollar bill. We are very valuable to God. He loves us dearly. And no matter how life has treated us (crumbled our spirit, spat on our self-worth, or stomped on our ideas and feelings), God knows how precious and worthwhile we are. He created us as valuable people worthy of the most wonderful praise and deserving of exquisite treatment. Nothing on this earth can change God's mind about us.

Wow! Too often we look at how we are treated and then somehow feel we deserve that kind of treatment. Some people tell us we have goofed. They point out our faults and even embellish the idea of how terrible those actions are. Then they proceed to treat us in a fashion that is unkind and thoughtless. Our concerns and problems mean nothing to them. How different God is in his thoughts and feelings about us.

But God, who is rich in mercy, because of the great love he had for us, even when we were dead in our transgressions, brought us to life with Christ (by grace you have been saved), raised us up with him, and seated us with him in the heavens in Christ Jesus, that in the ages to come he might show the im-measurable riches of his grace in his kindness to us in Christ Jesus. For by grace you have been saved through faith, and this is not from you; it is the gift of God; it is not from works, so no one may boast. For we are his handiwork, created in Christ Jesus for the good works that God has prepared in advance, that we should live in them. Ephesians 2:4–10

God's major concern is that we to join him in heaven to enjoy his ever-lasting love and blessings. He will provide strength and grace to help us in those times when life is not treating us well. It may be the burden of a lost job, reduction in retirement benefits, the death of friends and rela-tives, or the many other challenges that weigh us down. God reminds us to look to him, accept his grace and understanding, and carry on know-ing he is always beside us.

You who dwell in the shelter of the Most High, who abide in the shadow of the Almighty, say to the Lord, "My refuge and fortress, my God in whom I trust." God will rescue you from the fowler's snare, from the destroying plague, will shelter you with pinions, spread wings that you may take refuge; God's faith-fulness is a protecting shield. You shall not fear the terror of the night nor the arrow that flies by day, nor the pestilence that roams in darkness, nor the plague that ravages at noon. Though a thousand fall at your side, ten thou-sand at your right hand, near you it shall not come. You need simply watch; the punishment of the wicked you will see. You have the Lord for your refuge; you have made the Most High your stronghold. No evil shall befall you, no af-fliction come near your tent. For God commands the angels to guard you in all your ways. With their hands they shall support you, lest you strike your foot against a stone. You shall tread upon the asp and the viper, trample the lion and the dragon. Whoever clings to me I will deliver; whoever knows my name I will set on high. All who call upon me I will answer; I will be with them in distress; I will deliver them and give them honor. With length of days I will satisfy them and show them my saving power. Psalm 91:1–16

The value of the five-dollar bill has no relationship to it being neat and clean, smooth and orderly or being stepped on or picked up. It has worth because it is backed by the government and has a stated value imprinted on its surface, both front and back. We have value because God says we do. We are lovable because God proclaims he loves us unconditionally and we in turn should extend that love onto others. God cares about us no matter our physical or mental ability, faith or lack of faith, successes or failures, highs or lows. His love is constant. God has forever etched us on his heart and held in his loving hands.

See, upon the palms of my hands I have written your name; your walls are ever before me. **Isaiah 49:16**

For the Lord is good and his love endures forever, his faithfulness continues though all generations. Psalm 100:5

Life is not fair and can be cruel. Life can attempt to crumble us, spit on us, throw us away, and treat us as if we are worthless. But always remember your worth and value is undiminished by the world because God has created you in his image, making you more highly prized than possessions, status in society, or any five-dollar bill.

No, in all these things we conquer overwhelmingly through him who loved us. For I am convinced that neither death, nor life, nor angels, nor principalities, nor present things, nor future things, nor powers, nor height, nor depth, nor any other creature will be able to separate us from the love of God in Christ Jesus our Lord. Romans 8:38, 39

As the Father loves me, so I also love you. Remain in my love. If you keep my commandments, you will remain in my love, just as I have kept my Father's commandments and remain in his love. "I have told you this so that my joy may be in you and your joy may be complete. This is my commandment: love one another as I love you. No one has greater love than this, to lay down one's life for one's friends. You are my friends if you do what I command you. I no longer call you slaves, because a slave does not know what his master is doing. I have called you friends, because I have told you everything I have heard from my Father. It was not you who chose me, but I who chose you and appointed you to go and bear fruit that will remain, so that whatever you ask the Father in my name he may give you. This I command you: love one another. John 9:9–17

O God, you are my God—for you I long! For you my body yearns; for you my soul thirsts, like a land parched, lifeless, and without water. So I look to you in the sanctuary to see your power and glory. For your love is better than life; my lips offer you worship! Psalm 63:1–3

God Brings Color In to Your Life

God brings color into your life every day in many interesting and un-usual ways. Have you noticed lately?

Have you looked at the delicate and beautiful flowers in the store? Have you been attracted to the smell of the flowers in the garden or along the path to work? What about the hanging baskets at a business? What about the majestic rainbow that appeared after the rainstorm? Did you catch it? Have you noticed that God has provided you with vivid impressions, both physical and abstract, throughout your hectic week?

Better yet, have you been aware of the brilliance of the people you know, meet, and have a relationship with? Do you really appreciate what you have been given? Remember the terrific smile you received when you needed it most? What about the hug received from a relative or friend? Isn't that something colorful in your life?

God also had enriched your life with his church, sacraments, and word. Have you been taking advantage of them? When was the last time you drank in all the goodness they provide?

The canvas of life can be dull and boring or vibrant and exciting. God provides, but we have to be receptive. Take some time and appreciate what the Lord has prepared and openly shares with you. When you have done that, say thanks.

But you are a chosen people, a royal priesthood, a holy nation, a people belonging to God, that you may declare the praises of him who called you out of darkness into his wonderful light. 1 Peter 2:9

Clap your hands, all you nations; shout to God with cries of joy. Sing praises to God, sing praises; sing praises to our King, sing praises. For God is the King of all the earth; sing to him a psalm of praise. Psalm 47:1, 6, 7

God is Like a Convenience Store

God is like a convenience store. How? Well, God is very convenient to get to. He is just around the corner like those stores. God wants to be available to us so he has made is very easy to find him.

O people of Zion, who dwell in Jerusalem, no more will you weep; He will be gracious to you when you cry out, as soon as he hears he will answer you. Isaiah 30:19

Talk about service. God is just a thought and prayer away. Even 7–Eleven can't match that.

If we have any doubts about God's availability the Bible provides more examples.

Before they call I will answer; while they are still speaking I will hear. Isaiah 65:24

Call to me and I will answer you and tell you great and unsearchable things you do no know. Jeremiah 33:3

Then you will call upon me and come and pray to me, and I will listen to you. Jeremiah 29:12

Walgreens and 7–Eleven stores remind us they are open in case of an emergency whether it be a sore throat, a rash or some other problem. Just stop in and pick up what you need - it will be there. God reminds us that he also is there to help when spiritual emergencies or temporary problems come upon us.

Evening, morning and noon I cry out in distress and he hears my voice. Psalm 55:17

The Lord is a refuge for the oppressed, a stronghold in times of trouble. Psalm 9:9

Do not be anxious about anything, but in everything, by prayer and petition, with thanksgiving, present your requests to God. And the peace of God, which transcends all understanding, will guard your hearts and your minds in Christ Jesus. Philippians 4:6–7

Not only is God there, he knows exactly what we require. The convenience store has many items and the managers hope they have specifically what you require. But sometimes they are out of a particular product or they are waiting for another shipment to come in to the store. God is always available with what we need when we need it. His grace and blessings are never out of stock.

And my God will meet all your needs according to his glorious riches in Christ Jesus. Philippians 4:19

There is no want to them that fear him. They that seek the Lord shall not want any good thing. Psalm 34:9, 10

Then the Lord, your God, will increase in more than goodly measure the returns from all your labors, the fruit of your womb, the offspring of your livestock, and the produce of your soil; for the Lord, your God, will again take delight in your prosperity, even as he took delight in your fathers. Deuteronomy 30:9

Walgreens and 7–Eleven supply many services, but they cannot give guidance and support for many of our personal problems. God can.

I have the strength for everything through him who empowers me. Philippians 4:13

Yet will I rejoice in the Lord and exult in my saving God. God, my Lord, is my strength; he makes my feet swift as those of hinds and enables me to go upon the heights. Habakkuk 3:19, 20

For the Lord will be your confidence, and will keep your foot from the snare. Proverbs 3:26

God's word provides insights to many situations such as fear, physical sickness, financial problems, marital problems, and grief. As we read his word in the Bible and pray to him for assistance, we begin to deal with our difficulties. He will deliver to us the peace we need to manage or solve our problems.

Many Wal-Marts are now open twenty-four hours a day. They are trying to compete with convenience stores and the traditional department stores in providing us with their services and products. Their slogan states they are the "saving place." That slogan fits God to a T.

But when the kindness and generous love of God our savior appeared, not because of any righteous deeds we had done but because of his mercy, he saved us through the bath of rebirth and renewal by the holy Spirit, whom he richly poured out on us through Jesus Christ our savior, so that we might be justified by his grace and become heirs in hope of eternal life. Titus 3:4–7

We know that Wal-Mart, Walgreens, 7–Eleven and other stores plan to be everywhere we need them and attempt to provide solutions to most of our physical problems and also attend to some of our creature comforts. May we see these establishments and be reminded of the all encompassing love and compassion of God. May we recognize that he is just as convenient, takes care our physical needs, provides for our spiritual requirements, and also wants us to receive the most intimate desires of our heart. God plans for our salvation so we can enjoy the everlasting joy of heaven when we die. Not only that, he does not require us to have money or a credit card in order to receive his blessings.

And this is the will of the one who sent me, that I should not lose anything of what he gave me, but that I should raise it (on) the last day. For this is the will of my Father, that everyone who sees the Son and believes in him may have eternal life, and I shall raise him (on) the last day. John 6:39, 40

God is much more convenient than anything man can create. He is quicker and more efficient than the Internet. He never has a power failure, always has everything we need in stock, looks out for our best interests, and provides for our every need abundantly, all without cost or the need of newspaper fliers or store coupons. God runs and maintains the most exquisite cost free convenience store anywhere.

All you who are thirsty, come to the water! You who have no money, come, receive grain and eat; Come, without paying and without cost, drink wine and milk! Why spend your money for what is not bread; your wages for what fails to satisfy? Heed me, and you shall eat well, you shall delight in rich fare. Come to me heedfully, listen, that you may have life. Isaiah 55:1–3

God's Grocery Store

Shopping might be the biggest form of entertainment in the United States. People look for bargains, find unique items, and search for the best gift possible for a particular person. They spend much time searching, comparing, and buying.

How about going into God's grocery store, which makes all those malls, fancy stores, and unique boutiques look very ordinary? The best part is the fact that you don't have to leave home. The store is in your heart. Inside the store are enough wonderful things to meet all of your needs.

The aisle with the fruits of the spirit contains items like joy, peace, patience, and gentleness. The spirit's gifts in aisle two have the quality items of wisdom, knowledge, serving, teaching and leadership. Don't forget aisle three, which has Jesus—the bread of life. Each aisle is unique, has quality products, and is arranged to meet your various needs throughout your life.

Another feature of God's grocery store is that you get the unlimited use of the store's credit card. All charges have been prepaid by the death of Jesus. Each item is a free gift. What more could you ask for?

Reading God's word gets you the credit card. The credit card gets you into the store. Once inside the store, you can shop day or night, now and then, or all the time. The choice is yours. The options are endless, and the credit card never expires. Shopping, anyone?

Every good and perfect gift is from above, coming down from the Father of the heavenly lights, who does not change like shifting shadows. James 1:17

Praise be to the God and Father of our Lord Jesus Christ, who has blessed us in the heavenly realms with every spiritual blessing in Christ. For he chose us in him before the creation of the world to be holy and blameless in his sight. In love he predestined us to be adopted as his sons through Jesus Christ, in accordance with his pleasure and will—to the praise of his glorious grace, which he has freely given us in the one he loves. In him we have redemption through his blood, the forgiveness of sins, in accordance with the riches of God's grace that he lavished on us with all wisdom and understanding. Ephesians 1:3–8

"I am the living bread that came down from heaven. If anyone eats of this bread, he will live forever. This bread is my flesh, which I will give for the life of the world." John 6:51

God's Mercies

God's mercies are infinitely greater than any of our sins. Fr. Joseph Lombardo

Wow! Can that really be true? That would mean I no longer have any excuse why I shouldn't go to God's church, read his words, and practice loving myself and my neighbors. What a relief! But I still have many concerns and feelings of guilt.

I have lived a less than stellar life. I have been a carouser. I have treated people as objects to be used rather than people to love and to cherish. I have sought my own gratification instead of putting my efforts into helping others. I feel I am not worthy of worshiping God.

God's answer to that kind of logic is that his mercies are greater than any of our sins.

For I will forgive their evildoing and remember their sins no more. Hebrews 8:12

I have consistently cheated on my taxes, taking more deductions that I should and not declaring all of my income. I have not always been honest in my business dealings. Too often I have bent the truth to my advantage.

The Bible reveals to us something about God and his reaction to sin.

If we say, "We are without sin," we deceive ourselves, and the truth is not in us. If we acknowledge our sins, he is faithful and just and will forgive our sins and cleanse us from every wrongdoing. 1 John 1:8, 9

I would feel like a hypocrite if I went to church because of my feelings about other people's virtues and motives. I also don't want to face some of the people I have treated poorly. Surely I can't be forgiven for what I have done. I can't start over and I couldn't ever prosper again after what I have done.

But again God reacts differently than we do.

Bless the Lord, my soul; do not forget all the gifts of God, who pardons all your sins, heals all your ills, delivers your life from the pit, surrounds you with love and compassion, fills your days with good things; your youth is renewed like the eagle's. Psalm 103:2–5

What should I do to put my past sins into perspective with my current situation? How can I forget the past and move on? How do I change so I won't feel bad about my actions? How do I get rid of my guilt?

The Bible provides us with a prayer to God which answers our concerns about our past sins and the resulting guilt it leaves behind.

Have mercy on me, God in your goodness; in your abundant compassion blot out my offense. Wash away all my guilt; from my sin cleanse me. For I know my offense; my sin is always before me. Against you alone have I sinned; I have done such evil in your sight that you are just in your sentence, blameless when you condemn. True, I was born guilty, a sinner, even as my mother conceived me. Still, you insist on sincerity of heart; in my inmost being teach me wisdom. Cleanse me with hyssop, that I may be pure; wash me, make me whiter than snow. Let me hear sounds of joy and gladness; let the bones you have crushed rejoice. Turn away your face from my sins; blot out all my guilt. A clean heart create for me, God; renew in me a steadfast spirit. Do not drive me from your presence, nor take from me your holy spirit. Restore my joy in your salvation; sustain in me a willing spirit. Psalm 51:1–14

I feel better now. There are many examples in the Bible about God's love and forgiveness that show that if I really feel sorrow for my past, I can change my behavior and move beyond my sins and guilt feelings. Those past sins need not hold me back from receiving God's blessings, changing my life, and living life with abundance. Truly God's mercies are greater than any and all of my sins.

But if the wicked man turns away from all the sins he committed, if he keeps all my statutes and does what is right and just, he shall surely live, he shall not die. None of the crimes he committed shall be remembered against him; he shall live because of the virtue he has practiced. Ezekiel 18:21–22

Heaven is Like

After exhaustive research I have the answer to what heaven is really like. There are many kinds of the joys and feelings you will have upon reaching your celestial home. Here are some of them.

The joy in heaven will be one thousand times the joy you feel at a wedding here on earth.

I will praise you, Lord, with all my heart; I will declare all your wondrous deeds. I will delight and rejoice in you; I will sing hymns to your name, Most High. Psalm 9:1, 2

Whenever we have been to the doctor for tests and the results are good, we feel relieved. In heaven you will feel relief five hundred times greater than any relief you feel on earth.

I have brushed away your offenses like a cloud, your sins like a mist; return to me, for I have redeemed you. Raise a glad cry, you heavens: the Lord has done this; shout, you depths of the earth. Break forth, you mountains, into song, you forest, with all your trees. For the Lord has redeemed Jacob, and shows his glory through Israel. Isaiah 44:22, 23

We all have different intensities and kinds of our love for ourselves and others. The love you have as a parent for you child is great. Great also is your love for your spouse. The love you will feel in heaven will be twenty thousand times as great as your love on earth for your child or spouse.

O God, you are my God—for you I long! For you my body yearns; for you my soul thirsts, like a land parched, lifeless, and without water. So I look to you in the sanctuary to see your power and glory. For your love is better than life; my lips offer you worship! Psalm 63:1–3

The love of the Lord is not exhausted, his mercies are not spent; they are renewed each morning, so great is his faithfulness. Lamentations 3:22, 23

You are my God, I give you thanks; my God, I offer you praise. Give thanks to the Lord, who is good, whose love endures forever. Psalm 118:28, 29

If we attend a retreat or some other religious gathering we are always happy to be comfortable in the group. When we are at ease we are willing to share our story with those in attendance without fear of judgment or rejection. In heaven our comfort level will be five hundred times greater than anything we experience in this life.

My sheep hear my voice; I know them, and they follow me. I give them eternal life, and they shall never perish. No one can take them out of my hand. John 20:27, 28

Only goodness and love will pursue me all the days of my life; I will dwell in the house of the Lord forever. Psalm 23:6

We know that no one begotten by God sins; but the one begotten by God he protects, and the evil one cannot touch him. We know that we belong to God, and the whole world is under the power of the evil one. We also know that the Son of God has come and has given us discernment to know the one who is true. And we are in the one who is true, in his Son Jesus Christ. He is the true God and eternal life. 1 John 5:18–20

Since death and sin will be no more, only good will be available in heaven; only wonderful experiences will be there for us to enjoy. God will bestow on us the most intense forms of the most pleasant emotions we feel only on a limited basis here on earth. The list might include beauty, peace, security, trust, friendship, humor, devotion, satisfaction, and compassion. Surely those emotions will be magnified many times what we experience on earth.

Do I really know if joy in heaven will be five hundred times that of earth? No, I don't. But I do know that heaven will be far greater than anything I can imagine now, whether that is one hundred times or a one thousand times or ten thousand times more. I will be more than surprised by the magnificence and glory of heaven.

In my father's house there are many dwelling places. If there were not, would I have told you that I am going to prepare a place for you? And if I go and prepare a place for you, I will come back again and take you to myself, so that where I am you also may be. John 14:2, 3

What eye has not seen, and ear has not heard, and what has not entered the human heart, what God has prepared for those who love him. 1 Corinthians 2:9

For this reason they stand before God's throne and worship him day and night in his temple. The one who sits on the throne will shelter them. They will not hunger or thirst anymore, nor will the sun or any heat strike them. For the Lamb who is in the center of the throne will shepherd them and lead them to springs of life-giving water, and God will wipe away every tear from their eyes. Revelation 7:15–17

Holy Water Shoes

A woman took her little bottle of holy water from church and put drops of water in the shoes of her children. When asked why she did that, she replied that she wanted her children to be reminded that God was always walking with them. He was always at their side. Wherever they went and whatever they did, God was their constant companion.

Did you realize that in that car accident you were in that God was there to comfort and console you? He was there to calm your fears, renew your spirits, and bring you safely through the experience. God's help may have come in the form of an understanding police officer. It may have shown itself in your neighbor who lent you their extra car until yours was repaired. Or it may have manifested itself in the thoughts and concerns of your spouse and children. You were not alone in the accident. God was there right with you.

God was also walking with you when you moved to another state. He was present when you hired the movers. He was there in the well wishes of your family and friends who were sad to see you go. God was even evident in the safe trip you had to your destination. He was there to welcome you in your new situation through the friendly people who made your transition smoother than it might have been. God was there to celebrate with you when you found the church in which to praise and honor him.

In your trials God is walking with you. In your joys God is celebrating with you. God is present in the ordinary features of your life. He is closer to you than even holy water in your shoes, daily providing guidance, peace, and understanding. You are never without God's love and concern.

I will not leave you orphans; I will come to you. John 14:18

Even if my father and mother forsake me, the Lord will take me in. Psalm 27:10

I no longer call you slaves, because a slave does not know what his master is doing. I have called you friends, because I have told you everything I have heard from my father. It was not you who chose me, but I who chose you and appointed you to go and bear fruit that will remain, so that whatever you ask the Father in my name he may give you. This I command you: love one another. John 15:15, 16

Though the mountains leave their place and the hills be shaken, my love shall never leave you nor my covenant of peace be shaken, says the Lord, who has mercy on you. Isaiah 54:10

How Great Thou Art

Koala bear, kiwi, kangaroo, and platypus. What a wide variety of animals! Rose, coleus, lily, crocus, and ivy. What a fantastic arrangement of flowers and plants! Mountain, glade, brook, desert, and forest. Such an abundance of landscape!

Could it be God created the wildlife "down under?" Did God design the beautiful flowers and plants of America? What about the majestic mountains around the world? Surely the hand of God is in all of these!

O Lord my God, when I in awesome wonder
Consider all the works thy hand had made.
I see the stars, I hear the mighty thunder,
Thy pow'r throughout the universe displayed.

When through the woods and forest glades I wander
And hear the birds sing sweetly in the trees;
When I look down from lofty mountains grandeur
And hear the brook and feel the gentle breeze.

As great as that creation is, the most important thing that God did for us was to send his son to be our sacrificial lamb, to be our Savior. With that act we became heirs to the kingdom of heaven.

And when I think that God, his son not sparing,
Sent him to die, I scarce can take it in,
That on the cross my burden gladly bearing
He bled and died to take away my sin.

When Christ shall come with shout of acclamation
And take me home, what joy shall fill my heart!
Then I shall bow in humble adoration
And there proclaim: "My God, how great thou art!"

Then sings my soul, my Savior—God, to thee,
"How great thou art! How great thou art!"
Then sings my soul, my Savior—God, to thee,
"How great thou art! How great thou art!"

Song by John Newton

INRI

In his book *And the Angels Were Silent,* Max Lucado said of Jesus that "he would rather go to hell for you than go to heaven without you." You must be very precious in order for Jesus to think that. I like to think that the INRI written above Jesus on the cross stood for "I Never Regretted It." Jesus never regretted all the suffering he had to go through to save you and me.

When you catch yourself lying to someone, take time to think of Jesus being mocked and spat upon. Jesus would say to you, "I never regretted it."

When you get angry and jealous and use words that are hurtful, think of Jesus being whipped. Think of the pain he endured. Jesus would tell you, "I never regretted it."

The next time you join the group in making fun of others, think of Jesus hanging on the cross. Jesus's eyes would tell you, "I never regretted it."

You will sin and do things you are ashamed of in the future. You will make poor decisions that are not always Christian ones, and you will have to live with the results. But in each and every case Jesus still loves you. Jesus suffered and died for all your sins so you could join him in heaven. Jesus was perfect because you can never be perfect. Jesus became your scapegoat, the supreme sacrifice given to the father in your name. Jesus gave all of himself for you.

Take some time to thank Jesus for his sacrifice. Commit yourself to doing a better job of living a Christian life. Pray for guidance and strength to live that Christian life. Know that all your efforts will not gain you heaven. It was already bought for you because Jesus never regretted suffering and dying for you.

For God so loved the world that he gave his one and only son, that whoever believes in him shall not perish but have eternal life. John 3:16

It's Amazing

Use the maze to find out how special you are.

U	B	G	O	D	C	C	G
N	B	F	Q	L	H	H	W
C	T	R	K	O	B	R	F
O	Q	T	F	V	R	T	C
N	C	U	H	E	T	B	G
D	U	H	U	S	M	E	K
I	X	Z	O	N	Y	A	A
T	I	O	N	A	L	L	Y

The Lord appeared to us in the past saying: I have loved you with an everlasting love: I have drawn you with loving-kindness Jeremiah 31:3

Amen, amen, I say to you, whoever hears my word and believes in the one who sent me has eternal life and will not come to condemnation, but has passed from death to life. John 5:24

You are my God, I give you thanks; my God, I offer you praise. Give thanks to the Lord, who is good, whose love endures forever. Psalm 118:28, 29

For God so loved the world that he gave his only son, so that everyone who believes in him might not perish but might have eternal life. John 3:16

For by grace you have been saved through faith, and this is not from you; it is the gift of God; it is not from works, so no one may boast. Ephesians 2:8

Just?

I'm just a stay-at-home mom, a construction worker, an elementary teacher, an underpaid secretary, or a tired sales clerk.

But to God you are a wonderful stay-at-home mom who instructs and encourages the smallest and gentlest people in God's kingdom. To God you are a talented construction worker who provides for the needs of every facet of the community with housing that protects people from the dangers of nature. God sees you as a dedicated elementary teacher who creates an atmosphere of trust and fairness that helps young people form into thoughtful and caring adults. God sees an underpaid and talented secretary as the cornerstone of any business that relies on dedicated and professional people to make the business profitable and efficient. He also appreciates the tired and knowledgeable sales clerk who helps provide his people with the necessities of life. God wants his people not to worry about what they should wear or eat, but to concentrate on his tremendous love for them. The efficient sales clerk makes the time spent on necessities minimal, which allows people more time they can spend with their God.

When you tell people you are just this or that, you undermine God's love and devotion to you. He has showered you with all the gifts and talents you need to not only survive but to thrive in this world. You should appreciate your own special gifts without comparing them to others. The gifts of others are meant to complement your talents instead of being in competition with them. The world needs all kinds and degrees of gifts, and yours are no exception. Those talents are part of God's integrated, worldwide plan meant to help his people live life abundantly. Without your gifts being used to the benefit of others, the plan is incomplete.

Take time today to list the talents you see in yourself and the ones others have observed in you. Give thanks to God for his generosity in giving you those precious and unique gifts. Then ask, in prayer, for God's help in maximizing the size and scope of those gifts. Look at every day as an opportunity to share talents with the people you meet. Never let yourself get caught in the trap of saying you are just a secretary or a stay-at-home mom or any other description of your wonderful God-given talents.

Every good and perfect gift is from above, coming down from the Father of the heavenly lights, who does not change like shifting shadows. James 1:17

I, in the First Person

A conversation with Larry

I want to tell you three stories about different people. I will tell you them as if I am that person. See if you can tell what all three people have in common.

Story One

I am Jerry. I am an alcoholic. I was kicked out of school because I didn't fit in at all. I joined a local gang because my parents wanted nothing to do with me. They had given up because they thought I was unsalvageable.

That gang taught me how to survive. I learned to steal and lie very well. We celebrated our victories over society by having a drink. First one or two victory drinks and then more than two. Soon it was an entire bottle of booze at a time. It dulled the senses and took away the pain of my life for a while.

The gang stayed together for a year. But the more we drank the less dependable we became. We couldn't support each other with money or a meal or booze. We began to drift apart. I eventually found myself alone on the streets by day and in an alley by night. I was alone and miserable.

I may be miserable and alone, a drunk and a vagrant, but God loves me.

Story Two

I am Mary. I am a prostitute. I am only twenty, but I know every way to please a man sexually. I can do it all, and I have seen it all. Nothing is too strange or too weird. If it brings in money, I will do it.

On a great week I will make $1,500. On a bad week I will bring in $50. It all depends on the weather, the time of the year, and the strength of the economy. The better people are doing with money, the more willing they are to spend their money on me.

The place I live in is OK. It's a one bedroom with just a few pieces of furniture. The most expensive piece of furniture is the bed. It has a canopy with fancy lace and four posts. It really is elegant. I bought it when I had a really good month. It has to be terrific because it is where I make most of my money.

I worry about disease. But I have been lucky so far. I found a doctor who treats me without charging an arm and a leg. I have no insurance so I can't go in whenever I want to. It really has to be important or I don't go.

I wish I could find a man who likes me as a person and not a piece of meat. They look at me with such contempt. That really bothered me at first. Now I can ignore it and just be thankful I am getting paid.

This week I haven't worked because I am black and blue. The John I was working for refused to pay me the full amount. I let out a few choice words for him, and he didn't like it. He slapped me up pretty good. He said I should appreciate what he was doing for me. I was so ungrateful. So he taught me a lesson with his hands. I have to wait until the swelling goes down. Soon I can cover up the dark spots with makeup. Then I can earn some money again.

I hate this job! I hate me! I hate how I feel! I hate the world! But God loves me.

<u>Story Three</u>

I'm Allen. I am gay. I have AIDS. I found out I was gay when I was twelve. My parents thought I was disgusting. They couldn't look at me. I left them and the house when I was thirteen.

I went to a big city and found a sugar daddy. The man treated me well. I was like a little prince. I was cute. I was something to show off to his friends. I was somebody. I had nice clothes and did adult things like drinking and having sex. Life was good.

When I was about fourteen, "Daddy" found another young boy. He had both of us for a while. We were like brothers. But I began to see "Daddy" less and less. I didn't get to go to fine places anymore. My clothes were not the latest fashions. I suddenly had less spending money.

After a few months, "Daddy" decided he couldn't afford two boys. So he gave me $500 and kicked me out of the house. I was on my own.

I found some people to stay with for a while. They had been friends of "Daddy" and felt sorry for me. But they couldn't afford to take care of me either. So I got a job as a dish washer. I worked in that restaurant for a while but couldn't save any money because I was not on the payroll. In order to make more money I started selling my body, which brought in extra cash.

At age nineteen I was diagnosed with AIDS. I found out when I got a free blood test. The people at the clinic were nice. They treated me like a real person. They gave me suggestions, got me pamphlets to look over, and discussed places to get help.

But now what do I do? I can't go home. I can't go back to "Daddy." I have AIDS. I can't work without infecting someone else. I have no money and no hope. But God loves me.

<u>Larry</u>

All of these people have one thing in common—God loves them. How do I know? That's easy. Jesus said that the father was in him, and he was in the father. The father knows him, and he knows the father. God is love. God loves all of us just as Jesus loved us. He is the Good Shepherd who takes care of his sheep. Because of Jesus we are children of God. We are more valuable than birds. God knows even the hairs on our head. Even if our earthly mother forgets us, God won't.

We also know God loves us by the actions of his son, Jesus, who kept company with Matthew, the tax collector, and other sinners. Matthew was despised because he collected taxes for the Romans, who were the rulers over the Jewish nation. The Romans oppressed the Jews. Tax collectors were considered traitors by the Jewish people. Not only that, tax collectors usually lived very well because they exacted more money than they were supposed to collect. They often lined their pockets at the expense of the people. Yet Jesus kept company with Matthew. Why?

Jesus loved Matthew. Jesus looked beyond the exterior of the person and beyond the limitations of the man. Jesus saw the potential good in each human being. Jesus observed the child of God inside all of us, a loving creation of the father. His heart went out to all, no matter their station in life, their profession or ability. He loved unconditionally just like the father.

Jesus also spent time with prostitutes and adulterers. He told the woman at the well about her numerous husbands and the many errors she had made in her life. Instead of condemning her, he promised her living water, forgiveness, and a chance at a new life.

His great love looked beyond the failings of the person and saw the possibilities and future successes. Loved by Jesus, she was able to overcome evil and her shortcomings. Love could begin the process of change that would lead to the rebirth of the person to a healthier life, full of possibilities, wonders, and growth. Gone would be self-deception, self loathing, and destruction. Present in the person would be love, genuineness, self-worth, and growth.

Besides the prostitutes and adulterers, Jesus enjoyed the company of the weak and the abandoned. In his presence, unclean spirits were chased away. Diseased or broken bodies were made whole. Minds and hearts of people were opened. Instead of condemnation, Jesus offered them bread for the health of the body and spiritual food and drink for the nourishment of the soul. He offered them unlimited and unending love.

God, through Jesus, showered love on all the Jerrys, Marys, and Allens of his world. None were excluded. Jesus demonstrated his all-encompassing love to friend and foe alike. He offered the people new life filled with compassion and forgiveness. He became the sacrifice for all procuring redemption and eternal life for mankind.

God does not condone sin, accept evil, or encourage waywardness. But he does forgive our failings and provides the means for us to earn eternal life. Eternal salvation is not earned by our good deeds but by our faith in God and our willingness to serve him in the best way we can. Our past transgressions need not hold us back. God has seen every possible combination of sins, and he is always willing to help us change, encourage our improvement, and guide us with his love. What is past is past. But the future can be the difference between sin and death or love and eternal salvation. God's life-giving love is available to all people, no matter the race, color, sex, or past transgressions. No matter what happens in our life, we can always say with complete confidence, "But God loves me."

For God so loved the world that he gave his one and only son, that whoever believes in him shall not perish but have eternal life. John 3:16

The Lord appeared to us in the past, saying: I have loved you with an everlasting love; I have drawn you with loving-kindness. Jeremiah 31:3

May our Lord Jesus Christ himself and God our Father, who loved us and by his grace gave us eternal encouragement and good hope, encourage your hearts and strengthen you in every good deed and word. 2 Thessalonians 2:16, 17

I will heal their waywardness and love them freely, for my anger has turned away from them. Hosea 14:4

But because of his great love for us, God, who is rich in mercy, made us alive with Christ even when we were dead in transgressions—it is by grace you have been saved. And God raised us up with Christ and seated us with him in the heavenly realms in Christ Jesus, in order that in the coming ages he might show the incomparable riches of his grace, expressed in his kindness to us in Christ Jesus. Ephesians 2:4–7

Lord, may I learn to appreciate how truly gifted I am. Help me to grow and change into the person you meant for me to be. Help me to overcome any discouraging situations I encounter. May I always remember that no matter what happens to me in life that God loves me.

Oops

A bank in Binghamton, New York, had some flowers sent to a competitor who had recently moved into a new building. There was a mix-up at the flower shop, and the card sent with the arrangement read, "With our deepest sympathy."

The florist, who was greatly embarrassed, apologized. But he was even more embarrassed when he realized that the card intended for the bank was attached to a floral arrangement sent to a funeral home in honor of a deceased person. That card read, "Congratulations on your new location!
Taken from *Our Daily Bread Collector's Edition II.*

Oops! What a mistake. But what about our own life? Have we said things to people in haste or anger that we wish we could take back? Have we made plans and then with hindsight realized they were made with poor decisions on our part? How we regret those decisions! Have we done other things in our life that could have been done much better? We need to consider how much we had included God in our thoughts and plans at those times.

When we do things emotionally they often turn out poorly. When we don't pray about them we find we may have overlooked a much better solution. The less we take time to pray, the less chance God has to influence our decision and affect the outcome and the less chance there is for the situation to come to a positive conclusion. When things don't turn out the way we wanted them to, do we then complain that God was nowhere to be seen? How could God let that situation develop the way it did? It's simple. We didn't include God in our action, and he allowed us to reap the "benefits" of our decision.

In our daily lives we need to slow down, take our time, and include God in our decision making. If it is important in our life, then God wants to be there. If our choice could help determine our future situation, then God wants to help us take the best possible option. If we don't want to regret poor choices, then God needs to be included every step in the process. The more we pray and the more we let God be our guide, the better the chances are that the decisions we make will be well thought out and productive. It's our choice. We can include God and all his wisdom and grace or exclude him and rely on our own meager decision-making ability.

Not only has God promised to be with us, he has emphasized he will stand by us when we are thrust into a situation we have no control over or when we face things that are difficult or damaging to us. He will never abandon us. God will help us make wise decisions in our normal lives, and he will also stand by us in difficult times not of our own making. What a God he is!

Whether you turn to the right or to the left, your ears will hear a voice behind you saying, "This is the way; walk in it." Isaiah 30:21

For this God is our God forever and ever; he will be our guide even to the end. Psalm 48:14

Those who know your name will trust in you, for you, Lord, have never forsaken those who seek you. Psalm 9:10

Rock, Paper, Scissors

Remember the rock, paper, scissors game you played as a child? You had to choose which item you would be. Each choice had advantages and disadvantages. The winner would be allowed to inflict pain on the loser.

In our life we tend to be more like one thing than another. We may be like the rock: tough and unyielding or dependable and strong. We may be like the paper: brittle and thin but also intellectually and creatively useful. Great music and fantastic novels are not written on a rock or scissors. Or we may be like the scissors: sharp with the ability to cut and separate or pointed and unyielding.

In the game you had to choose one of the objects that you wanted to be. In real life we need to be more adaptable than the rock, scissors, or paper. When we need to be flexible, in order to shift from the rock to the scissors or from the scissors to the paper, God's help is essential. Through prayer and grace, we can change to meet our present circumstance.

God is strong like a rock, providing strength and durability. He is sharp like a scissors, providing insight to difficult situations. Like the paper, God's love is all encompassing, covering all our needs and desires.

When we have to be strong and unyielding like the rock, we should seek help from God who knows best how to provide all the toughness needed.

When our problems demand insight, we have God's words and sacraments to cut through the layers of our difficulties. In our brittle paper stages, God provides love for us, which will envelope the obstacle helping us solve the problem with creativeness and cleverness.

In this world of constant and frequent change, we need to be adaptable. With God at our side guiding us, we can be whatever the situation calls for. He alone can sustain us in all our changes from rock to paper to scissors and back to rock.

And my God will meet all your needs according to his glorious riches in Christ Jesus. Philippians 4:19

I can do everything through him who gives me strength. Philippians 4:13

If you remain in me and my words remain in you, ask whatever you wish, and it will be given you. John 15:7

In that day you will no longer ask me anything. I tell you the truth, my father will give you whatever you ask in my name. Until now you have not asked for anything in my name. Ask and you will receive, and your joy will be complete. John 16:23, 24

Somebody

You're nobody till somebody loves you. You're nobody till somebody cares. These words to an old song by Russ Morgan, Larry Stock and James Cavanaugh written in 1944 still ring true today. We are nobody till somebody loves us. It is great to know that God loves us. That loves makes us somebody important, somebody precious, somebody worth more than their weight in gold or precious jewels.

God's love for us makes all the difference. We have no chance to suc-ceed, no chance to have happiness, and no chance of salvation without the love of the Lord. His love is unconditional, everlasting, and life-giv-ing and is the only thing we need.

With God we have abundance, joy, and hope. Our faith in him provides us with the tools we need to survive in the world. We need to continue to thank God for being so generous, for loving us so, and for giving us the means to salvation and everlasting life.

What does God ask in return? We are to act justly, to love mercifully, and to walk humbly with our God.

The Lord your God is with you, he is mighty to save. He will take great delight in you, he will quiet you with his love, he will rejoice over you with singing." Zephaniah 3:17

May our Lord Jesus Christ himself and God our father, who loved us and by his grace gave us eternal encouragement and good hope, encourage your hearts and strengthen you in every good deed and word. 2 Thessalonians 2:16, 17

I will heal their waywardness and love them freely, for my anger has turned away from them. Hosea 14:4

For God so loved the world that he gave his one and only son, that whoever believes in him shall not perish but have eternal life. John 3:16

The Lord appeared to us in the past, saying: "I have loved you with an everlasting love; I have drawn you with loving-kindness." Jeremiah 31:3

Which Path?

George, a young man from a small town, went to the big city for a sexual adventure. Not knowing his way around the city, he went to the bus station to get some information. He went up to the ticket window and asked the elderly gentleman there where he could find some female companionship on an hourly basis.

The man smiled and told George where he could find the female associates. He indicated that George should take plenty of cash because the ladies did not take credit cards. He stated that the ladies would charge $500 and up for their companionship.

"Boy, sin is expensive," George blurted out.

"Oh, but there are some fringe benefits," stated the smiling ticket seller. "You get free feelings of shame and guilt. You also get a free chance at catching a sexually transmitted disease." He also suggested George might look elsewhere for his entertainment. Dejected, George left the bus station and headed back to the small town.

George's story should remind us of some of the decisions we have to make in our lives. We should also remember that sin is expensive, while God's love and grace is free. Sin is corrosive and destructive while God's love is uplifting and life-giving. Sin also causes death and eternal pain in hell while God's love leads us to eternal peace and joy in heaven.

During our life's adventures we will have many options. We can choose a path that leads to destruction and ruin through sin or we can choose the life-giving path that only God provides. We can accept the love offered free of charge from God or sin, which is expensive in this life and the next.

The Lord is with me to the end. Lord, your love endures forever. Never forsake the work of your hands! Psalm 138:8

We know that all things work for good for those who love God, who are called according to his purpose. Romans 8:28

For if you live according to the flesh, you will die, but if by the spirit you put to death the deeds of the body, you will live. Romans 8:13

Let no one have contempt for your youth, but set an example for those who believe, in speech, conduct, love, faith, and purity. 1 Timothy 4:12

Section Three:
Prayer

Prayer is communication with our God. We can glimpse it in nature. We can feel it in births and deaths we encounter. We find God in church, in our friends and relatives and acquaintances. The power of prayer can transform us into the person God created us to become. Prayer is free and available 24/7. Prayer is our way of getting to know God and developing a wonderful relationship with him.

This is the confidence we have in approaching God: that if we ask anything according to his will, he hears us. And if we know that he hears us—whatever we ask—we know that we have what we asked of him. 1 John 5:14, 15

Then you will call, and the Lord will answer; you will cry for help, and he will say: Here am I. Isaiah 58:9

This third I will bring into the fire; I will refine them like silver and test them like gold. They will call on my name and I will answer them; I will say, "They are my people," and they will say, "The Lord is our God." Zechariah 13:9

ALONE

"Let us pray for those who have no one to pray for them."

This prayer often voiced by Bev Karpfiner should cause us some concern. Are there people who feel so alone that they think no one cares for them much less prays for them? Are there people among us who don't fit in? Don't mingle? Have unusual ideas and practices? People who just "don't get it?" Of course there are. We all know one person who feels alone.

Isn't it sad that those people feel so isolated? Knowing we have a God who loves us dearly, even with all our human faults, should be encouraging. Maybe it's up to us to show the lonely people of the world though our actions that God loves them. What can we do to show them? It might be looking past the person's appearance or actions, to see one of God's favorite creations. It might be a simple hello or a pat on the back. Listening to their concerns can be very uplifting for them. There are all kinds of actions we can perform that show them they are valuable, unique, and children of God.

Don't forget to pray first. Pray for guidance from God. Pray for the courage to make the first step in integrating lonely people into the community. Start small. Do things that are simple, easy, and take little commitment. You might even get friends to join you. After a while expand your actions and commitment. God is by your side so you can relax in the knowledge that he is in control. You can invite and encourage, but not control what other people will do. Let God do the changing, while you do the inviting of the lonely person to be part of your community.

All that the father gives me will come to me, and whoever comes to me I will never drive away. John 6:37 Accept one another, then, just as Christ accepted you, in order to bring praise to God. Romans 15:7

Being Aware of the Presence of God

Have you ever felt too rushed to pray? Have you ever felt your prayers were ineffective? Have you ever been confused on which prayer you should use? Don't worry so much about the form and content of your prayers but be concerned only with being in God's presence.

How would you act with God next to you? Would your thinking process change if he was sitting by your side? Would you say things differently if you could see God's reactions? Realizing you are in God's presence will change your thinking, actions, and words. You can be in God's presence anytime and anywhere. You then can pray at all times, not just in church or when reading scripture in the privacy of your own home. You can be in constant communication with your God.

O people of Zion, who live in Jerusalem, you will weep no more. How gracious he will be when you cry for help! As soon as he hears, he will answer you. Isaiah 30:19

This is the confidence we have in approaching God: that if we ask anything according to his will, he hears us. And if we know that he hears us—whatever we ask—we know that we have what we asked of him. I John 5:14, 15

But when you pray, go into your room, close the door and pray to your father, who is unseen. Then your father, who sees what is done in secret, will reward you. And when you pray, do not keep on babbling like pagans, for they think they will be heard because of their many words. Do not be like them, for your father knows what you need before you ask him. Matthew 6:6–8

Then you will call upon me and come and pray to me, and I will listen to you. Jeremiah 29:12

Defects of Character

Lord, I ask you to guide me in getting rid of my defects of character. I will remember your words. I will seek your help. I will follow your voice.

I will give them a new heart and put a new spirit within them, I will remove the stony heart from their bodies; and replace it with a natural heart. Ezekiel 11:19-20

God Will Work In Me

I am confident of this, that the one who began a good work in you will continue to complete it until the time of Christ Jesus. Philippians 1:6

Thank you, Lord, for your work in me. Help me to rely completely on you and trust that your wonderful grace will be enough to change my heart, my routines, and my attitude. Amen.

Jonah's Prayer

From inside the fish Jonah prayed to the Lord, his God. He said:

The engulfing waters threatened me,
the deep surrounded me;
seaweed was wrapped around my head.
To the roots of the mountains I sank down;
the earth beneath barred me in forever.
But you brought my life up from the pit,
O Lord, my God.

Jonah 2:1, 5–7

God's help, guidance and grace are only a prayer away. With the help of God, let us not judge others. Let us also remember to ask for God's forgiveness if we do judge others unfairly. When we pray, let us be inclusive rather than exclusive. Let our prayers encompass all of God's people.

Jump Start

Instead of jump-starting your day with coffee, why not start with prayer? Imagine what would happen if you started out the day thanking God for his bountiful goodness. Imagine the way you would look at the events of the day when you started out by being positive. Would you react the same? Would things upset you easily? Would you treat other people with a smile? Start your day by praising God.

I will extol you, my God and king; I will bless your name forever. Every day I will bless you; I will praise your name forever. Great is the Lord and worthy of high praise; God's grandeur is beyond understanding. The Lord is gracious and merciful, slow to anger and abounding in love. The Lord is good to all, compassionate to every creature. All your works give you thanks, O Lord and your faithful bless you. Psalm 145:1–3, 8–10

After thanking God for goodness, take time to dedicate your day to the service of the Lord. Plan to be kind to others, praise them for their goodness, and help them when needed. Imagine the wonderful day you would have if all you did was dedicated in prayer to God.

Let love be sincere; hate what is evil, hold on to what is good; love one another with mutual affection; anticipate one another in showing honor. Do not grow slack in zeal, be fervent in spirit, serve the Lord. Rejoice in hope, endure in affliction, persevere in prayer. Contribute to the needs of the holy ones, exercise hospitality. Bless those who persecute (you), bless and do not curse them. Rejoice with those who rejoice, weep with those who weep. Have the same regard for one another; do not be haughty but associate with the lowly; do not be wise in your own estimation. Do not repay anyone evil for evil; be concerned for what is noble in the sight of all. If possible, on your part, live at peace with all. Beloved, do not look for revenge but leave room for the wrath; for it is written, "Vengeance is mine, I will repay, says the Lord." Rather, "if your enemy is hungry, feed him; if he is thirsty, give him something to drink; for by so doing you will heap burning coals upon his head." Do not be conquered by evil but conquer evil with good. Romans 12:10–21

Having thanked God for his goodness and many blessings and dedicated your day to him, take a little time to ask God for the grace you will need to accomplish your prayer goals. Knowing that God is with you will be a comfort. Remember, he does not require us to succeed in our tasks but only to put forth our best efforts. God will take our efforts and accomplish great deeds.

We know that all things work for good for those who love God, who are called according to his purpose. If God is for us, who can be against us? He who did not spare his own Son but handed him over for us all, how will he not also give us everything else along with him? Who will bring a charge against God's chosen ones? It is God who acquits us. Romans 8:28, 31–33

So jump start your day with prayer, and see what wonders you can accomplish with God's awesome grace and support.

Litany 2012

Lord, Creator of the universe.

    Holy God, I praise Thy name.

Lord, Creator of the Sun, Moon, and Sky.

    Holy God, I praise Thy name.

Lord, Creator of animals and plants.

    Holy God, I praise Thy name.

Lord, Creator of all humankind.

    Holy God, I praise Thy name.

God who provides justice and mercy for all.

    Lord, hear my prayer.

God who is protector of the poor and needy.

    Lord, hear my prayer.

God of wisdom, faith, trust, and love.

    Lord, hear my prayer.

God over time, space, life, and death.

    Lord, hear my prayer.

Lord, healer and sanctifier.

    Just say the word and my soul shall be healed.

Lord, God of house, city, nation, and world.

    Just say the word and my soul shall be healed.

Lord, God of forgiveness and renewal.
> Just say the word and my soul shall be healed.

Lord, guide, protector, encourager, and supporter.
> Just say the word and my soul shall be healed.

Lord, you are the creator of the universe. I praise your holy name. Lord, who hears our prayers, protects the poor, and provides wisdom, faith, and love, hear my prayers of petition and intercession. Lord, you are the healer, sanctifier, and king over house, city, nation, and world. Mend my hurts, both physical and spiritual, with your grace and guidance as I continue to daily grow and change as your loving child. Amen.

The Lord's Servant

Here is my servant whom I uphold,
  my chosen one with whom I am pleased,
Upon whom I have put my spirit;
  he shall bring forth justice to the nations.
                    Isaiah 41:1

Because you are precious in my eyes
  and glorious, and because I love you,
I give you honor.
  Do not be afraid—I am with you!
                    Isaiah 43:4, 5

Lord, because you are with me I am strong.

Lord, because you love me I am precious.

Lord, because you honor me I can do wonders.

Lord because of all you do for me I am not afraid and will endeavor to do your will in my own unique way. This I pray through Jesus Christ, our Lord. Amen.

O Gracious Lord

O Lord, thank you for:
The gift of your son who died so I can become a child of God and gain everlasting life.

O Lord, thank you for:
>The gift of [a person] who has shown me your love. A person who has inspired me and encouraged me to be the person you meant for me to be.

O Lord, thank you for:
>The gift of [an animal or bird] which is an example of your great abundance. You provided many animals and birds so I can see and appreciate your unlimited creativity.

O Lord, thank you for:
>The gift of plants. They help us to celebrate the miracle of Christ's birth, the joy of Easter morning, and the spectacle of your Liturgy. Their color, fragrance, and beauty enliven our praise and glory of your name.

Oh Lord, thank you for:
>The gift of me. Your love created me, sustained me in my trials, and celebrated my triumphs. You encouraged me to grow in

love in order to fulfill your designs of what I should become. Without you my life has no meaning. Because of you I am a gift, a one-of-a-kind creation, something special, a child of the most loving and caring God.

He who did not spare his own son, but gave him up for us all—how will he not also, along with him, graciously give us all things? Romans 8:32

So then, no more boasting about men! All things are yours, whether Paul or Apollos or Cephas or the world or life or death or the present or the future—all are yours, and you are of Christ, and Christ is of God. 1 Corinthians 3:21–23

Prayer for You and Me

As each new year begins, you can be renewed, recharged, and rejuvenated (or any other words you can use to describe the process of starting over). It can be a terrific time to decide to change yourself in one way or another. An excellent way to do that is to think outward to others—friends, people outside the neighborhood, people from outside the state, or even people from outside the country. We can have an effect on them by doing something for ourselves and for others. You can do this through prayer. Prayer is a powerful force which changes and renews. It can begin inwardly and proceed outwardly.

Remember, God does the changing, not us. But we can offer our prayer as a means of change. We can ask God to change us and those we meet through our prayers. God will be the guide and create the change.

Set aside time for prayer and offer those prayers to God to use in his time and manner. We need to make the commitment to reserve the time for prayer. Anyone can do it because we all have some time to give in the service of others.

Your prayers can be varied and suited to the talents you possess. Here are some suggestions:

Think of a person who needs prayer and every time you take a drink. Offer that up as prayer to God.

Reserve some time to **read the Bible** and offer that up to God.

Take time to practice **random acts of kindness** as a prayer.

Write a letter or make a **phone call** to specifically cheer someone up.

Create your own **poem** and dedicate it to God.

Give up something **(sacrifice)** and offer that up to God (chocolate for a day?).

Create a method to improve your area of weakness (be specific).

Use **music** as prayer (writing, listening, or singing).

Set aside some time each day to **talk and listen to God**.

Pray the **Our Father** or **Hail Mary** or the **Rosary** with a friend and offer that up to God.

Read a religious book, Bible commentary, etc.

These are only a few ideas on how to use prayer to help change yourself and others. Try to be inclusive with your prayers. Don't just pray for friends; pray for those you are having difficulties with, or even your enemies. Pray for the ability to forgive someone. Do not limit what God can do. Have a great year of prayer and renewal.

Prayer Is

Daily talking to God

Hi, God. I had a terrific morning. Thanks.

Singing God's praises

Any good Christian song will do. Just sing it and enjoy.

Asking God for help and guidance

Tell him your worries and fears, joys, whatever is important to you. Be yourself! Talk to him as a friend. God doesn't correct your grammar.

Reading God's letters to you

Read the Bible. It is God talking to you. Read it often. Read it in small groups, large groups, and on your own.

Writing poems, thoughts, and ideas

There are a zillion books and records for you to use to help you get closer to God. There is something just for you. Look for it and enjoy.

Telling God you love him

You can express your love for God in your own words, actions, and thoughts. Don't worry if you have the exact words. God knows your heart. Your talk can be short and sweet or long and involved - the choice is yours.

Thanks to Sr. Antoinette Hockerts for help in describing what prayer is.

Thank You, Lord

Thank you, Lord, for your gift of friends who bring companionship and joy into my life.

Thank you, Lord, for the animals and plants that are part of your wonderful universe.

Thank you, Lord, for the food that gives nourishment and refreshment to my body.

Thank you, Lord, for the difficulties in my life that help me grow and remind me of my need for you.

Thank you, Lord, for the gift of your son whose death and resurrection gives me eternal life.

Thank you, gracious Lord, for life and opportunities to praise your name. Amen.

Weak Prayer

Have you ever prayed for something very hard and for a long time, but what you prayed for didn't change? There could be several reasons for that situation that I would like you to consider.

The first problem might be in what you are praying to change or accomplish. Too often we want a particular problem solved in our time and in our way. Maybe you want your spouse or child to attend church and be involved in spiritual ventures. That doesn't seem to change even though you fervently pray for a turnabout in the situation. God might have some different ideas or avenues of change for your spouse or child. You may need to adapt the scope of your prayer.

State the problem to God. Then, instead of praying for him to change the situation to one you will be satisfied with, pray for God to provide whatever change is necessary to bring about peace and harmony for you. What can you do to make the situation better? How can you change to provide support for your loved ones without nagging and pressure? How can you get out of the way and allow God to work?

When we don't limit God to what he can do, changes occur that are beneficial to all those involved. Maybe your loved ones will not become full and active members of your church. Maybe they will join another denomination. Maybe they will start to find comfort in Scripture or other books on spirituality. Maybe they will become involved in church through some avenue you have not considered. Those might be changes God is working on but we don't consider a solution to our problem. If we bind God in our prayer to a particular solution, our prayer is very weak and has little power to cause change.

If we permit God to work on the problem (as if we have any control over God anyway) comfort and change will happen. Adjustment will happen, if slowly, to our people of concern. We can receive comfort knowing that God is in control, has heard our prayer, and is working on the circumstances. Our part in this equation is to pray, get out of the way, relax, and allow God to be productive.

A second problem that might cause weak prayer is our style and attitude. Our attitude must be that God will work and will work perfectly. We must turn our worries over to God knowing that he will work in his time and his way. We always have to remind ourselves that we are only intermediaries, and God is the one who creates wonders. We must pray and allow God to use that prayer in whatever manner he sees fit and surrender all control over the situation to him. Our attitude needs to be checked frequently. If we need help in releasing our control, we can also pray for that to happen.

If our attitude is right with God, sometimes the problem might be in the prayer we use. Prayer is wonderful, powerful, and useful but can be limited because we do the prayer by rote, saying the prayers without much effort and feeling. When that happens, I think prayer loses some of its dynamic properties. If you find you are zipping through prayer without any thought or many other thoughts seem to crowd out prayer, then you might want to change the prayer. Do a spontaneous prayer. Alter your prayer by adding your name or the person you are praying for and the situation you want changed. An example in the Our Father would be to change it to "Give us this day Tom's daily bread." Adjusting the pace of your prayer or emphasizing different words can be effective. Say the words out loud instead of in the silence of your mind. Vary your payer with a quote from a Psalm or some other familiar quote. Find a song that conveys your concerns and sing that song as part of your prayer. Any of these methods (or all) could help you keep your prayer honest, meaningful, and active.

One other thing you could consider is that some problems will require a lifetime or many lifetimes to solve. You may need to pray continuously during your life on earth, and then others will need to carry on those petitions. Some solutions will take a very long time to complete. In those cases your job is to be faithful, not get discouraged, pray, and again permit God to be God. Prayer is never wasted and always provides some form of change or relief. Even if you don't see any betterment in the situation, rely on God who tells us he cares and always listens to our concerns and responds to our prayers.

To avoid weak prayer, remember to allow God to use our prayers as he sees fit and have faith that God will use our prayers for good. Keep your mind and heart attentive in your prayers, and relax because you don't have to be in control of the situation for it to change. Pray always with sincerity and fervor and remember, "A week without prayer makes one weak."

Ask and it will be given to you; seek and you will find; knock and the door will be opened to you. For everyone who asks, receives; and the one who seeks, finds; and to the one who knocks, the door will be opened. Which one of you would hand his son a stone when he asks for a loaf of bread, or a snake when he asks for a fish? If you then, who are wicked, know how to give good gifts to your children, how much more will your heavenly father give good things to those who ask him. Matthew 7:7–11

At dawn let me hear of your kindness, for in you I trust. Show me the path I should walk, for to you I entrust my life. Rescue me, Lord, from my foes, for in you I hope. Teach me to do your will, for you are my God. May your kind spirit guide me on ground that is level. For your name's sake, Lord, give me life; in your justice lead me out of distress. Psalm 143:8–11

O God, you are my God—for you I long! For you my body yearns; for you my soul thirsts, like a land parched, lifeless, and without water. So I look to you in the sanctuary to see your power and glory For your love is better than life; my lips offer you worship! I will bless you as long as I live; I will lift up my hands, calling on your name. My soul shall savor the rich banquet of praise, with joyous lips my mouth shall honor you! When I think of you upon my bed, through the night watches I will recall that you indeed are my help, and in the shadow of your wings I shout for joy. My soul clings fast to you; your right hand upholds me. Psalm 63:1–9

Wireless Communication

The ultimate in wireless communication: prayer. This highway sign on the way to Door County, Wisconsin, reminds us to pray when we are happy. We should pray when we need help and support. We should pray when we need direction in our lives. We should pray when we are thankful. When we are lonely, we should pray. When others need help, we should pray.

There is no bad or right time to pray. There is no magic length to prayer. Prayer is the ultimate example of thoughtfulness, love, and communication.

Pray at the beginning of the day. Take time to pray at the end of the day. Continue to pray during the middle part of the day. Stop praying only when you have received all that you want and need and the wants and needs of the people around you are met completely.

But when you pray, go into your room, close the door and pray to your father, who is unseen. Then your father, who sees what is done in secret, will reward you. Matthew 6:6

If you, then, though you are evil, know how to give good gifts to your children, how much more will your Father in heaven give good gifts to those who ask him! Matthew 7:11

The righteous cry out, and the Lord hears them; he delivers them from all their troubles. Psalm 34:17

If we confess our sins, he is faithful and just and will forgive us our sins and purify us from all unrighteousness. 1 John: 9

If my people, who are called by my name, will humble themselves and pray and seek my face and turn from their wicked ways, then will I hear from heaven and will forgive their sin and will heal their land. 2 Chronicles 7:14

Your Words Are Spirit and Life

Your words are spirit and life, O Lord: richer than gold, stronger than death. Your words are spirit and life, O Lord; life everlasting. Bernadette Farrell

If God's words are spirit and life, why don't we spent time reading and digesting them? If the Bible is God breathed, why don't we find it an indispensable read? How come so little of our time and effort is spent reading the words which lead us to salvation and life everlasting? Why is the bible hidden away and not prominently placed in our living room? *All scripture is given by inspiration of God, and is profitable for doctrine, for re-proof, for correction, for instruction in righteousness. 2 Timothy 3:16 For the word of God is quick, and powerful, and sharper than any two-edged sword, piercing even to the dividing asunder of soul and spirit, and of the joints and marrow and is a discerner of the thoughts and intents of the heart. Hebrews 4:12 Every word of God is pure: he is a shield unto them that put their trust in him. Proverbs 30:5*

Is TV whether it be a soap opera, a crime investigation program or the latest American Idol, more important than God's precious gift to you? *For God so loved the world, that he gave his only begotten son, that whosoever believes in him should not perish, but have everlasting life. John 3:16*

If God's gift is the best present we could get, shouldn't we know as much about the giver as possible? We spend time looking at statistics for sports events to figure out who will win the big game. Why don't we find out some of the specifics about our salvation by reading the Bible? If it is important to know the background information about sports to know who will win the next game shouldn't the Bible be read daily to discover how we should understand, live and enjoy the game of life? *I will instruct you and show you the way you should walk, give you counsel and watch over you. Psalm 32:8 I will lead the blind on their journey; by paths unknown I will guide them. I will turn darkness into light before them, and make crooked ways straight. Isaiah 42:16*

If we are going to miss our favorite TV program because of work or another commitment don't we make sure we copy the show or find some way to view it later? Reading God's words should take at least as much of our effort as copying a show or renting a DVD. *Do not let your hearts be troubled. You have faith in God; have faith also in me. In my father's house there are many dwelling places. If there were not, would I have told you that I am going to prepare a place for you? And if I go and prepare a place for you, I will come back again and take you to myself, so that where I am you may be. John 14:1-4*

God's word is available to you at all times. It is not scheduled like a TV program, a movie, a football game, or some exciting special event. It does not depend on a satellite dish. Its reception doesn't require clear weather. It is not restricted because of black-out dates or sold out stadiums. Once it is accepted, it doesn't require a purchase agreement or extended guarantee. The purchase of God's word in the Bible are minimal but the rewards are heavenly. *Make known to me your ways, Lord; teach me your paths. Guide me in your truth and teach me, for you are God, my savior. Psalm 25:4-5*

When you are on vacation read your Bible. When you are resting at home pick up God's words for strength and guidance. If you are at the market take a breather to pray a psalm you memorized from the Old Testament. Between football games take some time to revel in God's letters to you. At the beginning of the day and before you sleep delve into the many words of comfort God provides to you in scripture. God has given us the Bible to learn about him, increase our faith, and to provide us strength to overcome any struggles. God is patiently waiting for us to read the Bible so he can bestow on us his words which are spirit and life. *Seek, the Lord while he may be found, call him while he is near. Isaiah 55:6 For just as from the heavens the rain and snow come down and do not return there till they have watered the earth, making it fertile and fruitful, giving seed to him who sows and bread to him who eats, so shall my word be that goes forth from my mouth; It shall not return to me void, but shall do my will, achieving the end for which I sent it. Isaiah 55:10-11*

Section Four:
Spiritual Growth

We experience spiritual growth when we let the Creator, Healer, and Lover God into our life. As we get to know our Savior, we try to emulate his characteristics and we change into a more perfect human being. Our interactions with others evolves appropriately because the Lord of Lords guides us, encourages us, and blesses us. Our Rock protects us in our earthly endeavors. The Prince of Peace acknowledges our efforts and will not let us falter, providing us with peace of mind to lighten our daily tasks. The more we rely on our Teacher and Everlasting Father the fuller our lives become today and in the future. Whatever we do, God is our hope, completeness, and perfection.

If any of you lacks wisdom, he should ask God, who gives generously to all without finding fault, and it will be given to him. James 1:5

You will understand the fear of the Lord and find the knowledge of God. For the Lord gives wisdom, and from his mouth come knowledge and understanding. He holds victory in store for the upright, he is a shield to those whose walk is blameless. Proverbs 2:5–7

For God, who said, "Let light shine out of darkness," made his light shine in our hearts to give us the light of the knowledge of the glory of God in the face of Christ. 2 Corinthians 4:6

Do not let this Book of the Law depart from your mouth; meditate on it day and night, so that you may be careful to do everything written in it. Then you will be prosperous and successful. Have I not commanded you? Be strong and courageous. Do not be terrified; do not be discouraged, for the Lord your God will be with you wherever you go. Joshua 1:8, 9

Abundance

5 loaves of bread + 2 fish + God's blessings = abundance

Whenever we call upon God, he answers. It is not always in the form or timeframe that we would like, but God always answers prayers.

When we pray we need to ask God for whatever we want, but we need to add to our prayer that the favor we ask for is for our own good and encouragement. That puts us in the right frame of mind to accept whatever God chooses to provide for us. That allows us to be grateful for whatever comes our way because we know and trust that God will provide for us because he is our loving father.

When we allow God to act with no expectations, we will be amazed at God's generosity and abundance. Do you remember when you had given up on a project and in frustration turned over the outcome to God? What happened was an outcome that was unexpected and much better than what you had anticipated. If God can bless two fish and a few loaves of bread and feed over five thousand people, imagine what he can do for us if we just have faith in his judgment and generosity. We need to get ourselves out of the way, allow God to work as only God can, and wait for the results. The results may be different than what we wanted, but they will be divinely inspired and full of abundance.

Another of his disciples, Andrew, Simon Peter's brother, spoke up, "Here is a boy with five small barley loaves and two small fish, but how far will they go among so many?" Jesus said, "Have the people sit down." There was plenty of grass in that place, and the men sat down, about five thousand of them. Jesus then took the loaves, gave thanks, and distributed to those who were seated as much as they wanted. He did the same with the fish. When they all had enough to eat, he said to his disciples, "Gather the pieces that are left over. Let nothing be wasted." So they gathered them and filled twelve baskets with the pieces of the five barley loaves left over by those who had eaten. John 6:8–13

Therefore I tell you, whatever you ask for in prayer, believe that you have received it, and it will be yours. Mark 11:24

Those who love me I also love, and those who seek me find me. With me are riches and honor, wealth that endures, and righteousness. My fruit is better than gold, even pure gold, and my yield than choice silver. On the way of righteousness I walk, along the paths of justice. Granting wealth to those who love me, and filling their treasuries. Proverbs 8:17–21

A Grain of Wheat

I tell you the truth, unless a grain of wheat falls to the ground and dies, it remains only a single seed. But if it dies, it produces much fruit. John 12:24

In our lives we have many deaths: the death of a loved one, the death of a career, the death of a relationship, the death of a cherished idea. All these deaths put a strain on our faith and endurance. But it is also a chance to grow, change, and produce much good. Pray that God pulls us through the death experience and that he may renew us afterward, creating abundant life where there was once loss and sorrow.

Lord, help us to accept the challenges in our lives. Help us to sustain our faith, nourish our souls, and renew our spirits. Lead us to a better understanding of you and acceptance of your will. With your help we will rise from the experience to produce more fruit for your glory. We pray this through Jesus Christ, Our Lord. Amen.

Alleluia, Praise the Lord.

Alleluia, Praise the Lord. Alleluia, Praise the Lord. Alleluia, Praise the Lord, Right Where We Are. Diane Davis.

The words to this song should remind us that our gifts and talents come from God. We cannot take credit for our gifts. We cannot boast of our talents. We cannot point in pride to our accomplishments. All our successes are God given.

We often see and hear athletes boast how fantastic they are, how they are the best, how they contribute to success more than others, how they are invaluable to their team. We need to pause. We should realize that all of those feats are allowed by a gracious and generous God. Without him, those fantastic contributions would not exist.

We too are guilty of being ungrateful to God. We often bask in our own accomplishments. We think we have done well and should be appreciated for our efforts because they are so stellar. We sometimes gloat when others don't measure up to us.

How foolish we can be. How ungrateful we can be. How self-centered we can be. It is easy. We are human and can easily fall into the devil's trap of believing in our own greatness. We sometimes are even guilty of false modesty.

We should constantly thank God for our good fortune. We should praise him for his generosity. We should realize that God is the giver of all good gifts and give him the glory for the wonderful things that happen in our lives.

The next time we have accomplished something we should take time to praise the Lord right where we are. *For the kingdom, power and glory are yours. Forever and ever. Amen.*

All of a Sudden

Here comes Peter Cottontail hoppin' down the bunny trail. Bang! Peter's dead!

Wow! What an unforeseen ending to a familiar children's song. It seems to come from nowhere. It is unexpected and unprepared for, tragic and confusing. What happens next? How should we react? Could we have been prepared for such an ending?

Isn't life like that? We hear of accidents that suddenly upset our whole world. If we are involved we may sustain injuries or trauma from the ordeal. We may be permanently changed in our bodily makeup. We may even be killed. Or the accident could happen to a close relative of ours. What then? What do we do? How do we respond?

Life has the possibility of sudden and drastic changes, and we need to be prepared for the unexpected. First of all we need to pray, communicating with our God daily learning who we are, what we should become, and how best we can serve our Lord. That happens best when we interact with God on a regular basis. We learn about God through his word, and from there we discover how we should be and act. The more we become the person we were designed to be, the more we will do the will of God.

Besides prayer, we need to attend liturgy, receive the sacraments, and study our faith through books and music. Retreats and contemplation enable us to discover God and his message for us. Getting involved in some ministry at church will also motivate us to grow spiritually. We can discover many ways to develop into a devout and active Christian in our parish.

If we do those things mentioned above, then we will be prepared for whatever happens in our lives, the ordinary and the extraordinary. If we are injured and become sick, we will have the background needed (from our prayers and active participation in our church) to thrive after the ordeal. We are assured that God will continually and willingly provide for our needs.

If we should die, we will be ready for the promised life in heaven. We will know we have done all that was expected of us by God. Our Lord will then provide us with the keys to the everlasting kingdom, welcoming us personally with open arms, a smile on his face, and a heart full of infinite love.

It's never too late to start a new beginning. The sooner we start, the faster we will be on the path God has designed for us, and the better prepared we will be for the unexpected. We won't worry, even if, like Peter Cottontail, we meet an untimely end. Don't waste a minute more. Start praying and meditating right now. Begin to work on your preparation for the unexpected, remembering God has promised to be with us every step of our journey. Relax and enjoy the marvelous adventure that awaits you.

I will lavish choice portions upon the priests, and my people shall be filled with my blessings, says the Lord. Jeremiah 31:14

Moreover, God is able to make every grace abundant for you, so that in all things, always having all you need, you may have an abundance for every good work. As it is written: "He scatters abroad, he gives to the poor; his righteousness endures forever." 2 Corinthians 9:8, 9

The Lord is my shepherd; there is nothing I lack. In green pastures you let me graze; to safe waters you lead me; you restore my strength. You guide me along the right path for the sake of your name. Even when I walk through a dark valley, I fear no harm for you are at my side; your rod and staff give me courage. Psalm 23:1–4

Which one of you would hand his son a stone when he asks for a loaf of bread, or a snake when he asks for a fish? If you then, who are wicked, know how to give good gifts to your children, how much more will your heavenly Father give good things to those who ask him. Matthew 7:9–11

Attitude

Maria age 12 wondered how would angels announce Jesus' birth today? The angel might appear before homeless people because they are not rich important people. The angel might say Jesus had been born in a shack, a tent, or an apartment.

This answer from *Kids Talk about God* by Carey Kinsolving and friends should remind us to look at our attitude. Do we dismiss other people because of their looks, clothes, odor, or position? Do we ignore others because they are less refined in their actions than we are? Do we discount another's suggestions because they don't speak in the manner we do? Is our attitude one that is accepting or one that excludes others? Does our attitude match that of Jesus?

If we say yes to any one of these questions, maybe we need to look more closely at our attitude toward others. Can we be more Christian in our dealings with people different than us? Can we be more caring? Where can be begin to change our attitude? How will we go about changing our attitude?

If Christ's birth was announced by angels to the lowly shepherds, can we ignore those less fortunate than us? We need to take time to analyze our attitudes, see where they are in opposition to God's call to love, and then work to change them into a more loving and accepting response to others. It is a lifetime project, one that will take a tremendous amount of prayers and God's free and constant encouragement and support to be successful.

In everything I did, I showed you that by this kind of hard work we must help the weak, remembering the words the Lord Jesus himself said: "It is more blessed to give than to receive." Acts 20:35

If anyone has material possessions and sees his brother in need but has no pity on him, how can the love of God be in him? 1 John 3:17

For I was hungry and you gave me something to eat, I was thirsty and you gave me something to drink, I was a stranger and you invited me in, I needed clothes and you clothed me, I was sick and you looked after me, I was in prison and you came to visit me. Matthew 25:35, 36

Beautiful Dreamer, Wake Onto Me. Starlight and Dewdrops are Waiting for Thee.

The words to the last song written by Stephen Foster can be a reminder to us. Sleeping and dreaming can be a opportunity to know God and his will for us. How? During rest we eliminate the many clamorous thoughts and ideas of our day. Getting rid of those thoughts gives God, in the form of the Holy Spirit, a chance to talk to us.

The Holy Spirit can communicate to us in many ways: through the Bible, Sunday sermons, spiritual writings, songs, signs and symbols. God's power and majesty can also be communicated to us by observing nature. The seasons, animals, plants, and human life all attest to the fantastic ability and creativity of our God. Friends, through their faith and actions, are another means the Holy Spirit uses to chat with us.

If that isn't enough, and as humans sometimes we want more proof of God and his goal for us, God provides us another opportunity to know him and his will. Being quiet, relaxed, and open to the Spirit's call happens while we sleep. During slumber some of the distractions of daily life can be forgotten allowing God to speak to us in a whisper.

When we have the sudden and unexplained urge to do something, when we have the feeling that we should do this or that, it is the Holy Spirit communicating to us. We need to be receptive to the message. We can only do that if we believe God, through the Holy Spirit, can direct and guide us, and we are willing to receive the message. Don't let this personal form of interaction with God go unheeded. Listen to and act on the Spirit's urging during sleep and in our quiet times

But the wisdom that comes from heaven is first of all pure; then peace-loving, considerate, submissive, full of mercy and good fruit, impartial and sincere. James 3:17

Bedtime Prayer

Now I lay me down to sleep:
I pray the Lord my soul to keep.
If I should die before I wake,
I pray the Lord my soul to take.
And this I ask for Jesus's sake.
Amen.

How many times we have said this prayer as a child before going to sleep? Do we really believe it? Are we ready to die now? Well, maybe not just right now. Maybe after a few more years of living. Maybe when I am old. Maybe after the children are grown. Maybe if I am sick or incapacitated in some way. Then I will be ready.

As humans, we cling to life. As Christians we should be ready to die and be eager to go to the place the Father has prepared for us.

If death can come at any minute, shouldn't we be equipped to die? How do we do that— live life, but be prepared to die? Pray for guidance from God. Pray for faith from the Father. Pray for wisdom from the Holy Spirit. Pray constantly. Keeping God in our thoughts will train us to accept whatever comes. Keeping God in our thoughts will help us live each precious moment as if it was our last. If we live each moment that way death will not be something to be feared, but rather a bridge to something better: eternal life with our loving God.

You will pray to him, and he will hear you, and you will fulfill your vows. Job 22:27

God is our refuge and strength, an ever-present help in trouble. Therefore we will not fear, though the earth give way and the mountains fall into the heart of the sea, though its waters roar and foam and the mountains quake with their surging. Psalm 46: 1–3

Busy

This is the Day the Lord has made, let us rejoice and be glad in it. Psalm 118:24

I have laundry to do. My doctor's appointment is today. The bedrooms and the kitchen have yet to be cleaned. Oh, the garbage hasn't been taken out. Mary has volleyball practice, and Scott has soccer practice. They both have to be dropped off. I also promised to provide a cake for the church bake sale. I am just too busy.

Yes, you are if you have a day or days with the likes of the one above. God has never intended us to be that busy. Is it necessary to be that busy to feel fulfilled? Before you answer that, consider some of the school shootings we have had. Many have been committed by kids from "good families." That means they have all the material things they need. They have a fine house, good clothes, and plenty of spending money. They are busy. They should have been happy, but they weren't. Why?

Having possessions doesn't cause one to have self-worth. Having the latest clothes doesn't make a person confident. Being involved in many activities doesn't guarantee high self-esteem. Going from one sport to another doesn't always provide spiritual meaning in one's life.

Being busy doesn't guarantee us anything except that we will have little free time. We need free time to spend together with our families. That quality time with parents and sisters and brothers can build confidence, self-worth, and a support system for a young person. That bonding is essential to build well-rounded people, both children and adults.

Being too busy means we often exclude God. Our Lord becomes an "add–on," something to fit in a crowded schedule rather than a source of inspiration and hope. Without God a conscience is not fully developed, and moral decisions are based on popular culture and ideas, which often leads to poor choices and disastrous results.

When our schedule becomes crowded, we often don't develop meaningful relationships with others. We have little or no support system. Not only that, we often treat others superficially and get the same response from others. So we have no support from family, friends, and most of all, God. What are the results? Name calling, taunting, date rapes, shootings, and suicides are just a few ramifications of being too busy and not taking the time to develop meaningful relationships.

We need to start looking at our life carefully. Where can we slow down? What can we drop and replace with quality time with God, family and friends? What efforts do we want to pursue, and which ones do we want to eliminate? With God's help we will change our life and make needed improvements. Our priorities will change, and happiness will increase until one day we can celebrate each and every wonderful day that the Lord has made for us.

Called to Be

Before I was born the Lord called me; from my birth he has made mention of my name. Isaiah 49:1

God calls us to be ourselves.

> We are called to value, celebrate and enjoy the gifts and talents he has given us.

God calls us to grow into ourselves.

> With his help, through his word and sacraments, we are called to grow, develop and change - to become what he knows we can be.

God calls us to grow out of ourselves.

> We are created to share our graces and talents with others. We are to help others in need and to spread the Good News of his love for us.

Tombo

This is what the Lord says—your Redeemer, the Holy One of Israel. "I am the Lord your God, who teaches you what is best for you, who directs you in the way you should go." Isaiah 48:17

Celebrate God

I knew a woman once whose body was degenerating. One thing after another needed repair. The poor lady was in constant pain. When visiting her in the hospital, she continually made fun of her agony and operations. I was impressed with her courage and spirit.

Later she decided to marry a man who was also in poor health. I couldn't imagine why she would get married. He wouldn't live very long, so why bother with a wedding and planning a future together? Within a year of the marriage, the man had indeed died. So why did she bother to get married?

I now think she married because she was in love, and she was determined to celebrate life for as long as she could and wherever she could. She was going to celebrate the joyful times in her life and rely on God to carry her through the difficult times.

How much more we, in good health, should celebrate the gift of life! We should give thanks to God for all the wonderful people and events he has provided for us. If we included God in all that we do, our lives and attitudes would change. We would have reason to be joyful, no matter what our current situation. His love and we, in turn, would touch the lives of those people around us.

We can learn to appreciate the moment. The past is gone, and the future has not yet come to pass, so celebrate the present. Live for the moment. Be a here and now person. If you celebrate God with your hands, your voice, and in all that you do, then God will be with you.

I lift up my eyes to the hills—where does my help come from? My help comes from the Lord, the Maker of heaven and earth. Psalm 121:1, 2

And we, who with unveiled faces all reflect the Lord's glory, are being transformed into his likeness with ever-increasing glory, which comes from the Lord, who is the Spirit. 2 Corinthians 3:18

Church Signs

Forbidden Fruit, Creates Many Jams.
If God Seems Far Away, Guess Who Moved?
Going the Wrong Way? God allows U Turns.
Love the Wedding, Invite Me to the Marriage . . . God.
WWW.ChristianityOasis.com

We have many messages bombarding us during our hectic days and nights, and too often we let those messages bounce off of us. We don't let the idea behind the messages sink into our consciousness. We need a method to help us decide which messages are worthwhile and which ones are not.

We should choose the method that puts God at the center. The method asks, "What would God want us to do? How does God want our life to change? In what direction does he intend for us to go?" Using this method as our filter, we can easily decide which messages we need to incorporate into our lives and which ones to ignore. If it is God centered, pay attention to the information. If it is not rooted in Godly ideas or principles, then ignore it.

Looking at the church signs, we can just hear God talking to us. ***God has supported his church and its people for over 2,000 years***. How active are we in his church? Where can we get more involved? In what areas can we

144

influence others to become active? What things are we doing now that prevent us from being more involved in God's church? What activities can we do that will inspire others before we expire?

As one sign states, we are not so good we can keep away from church. We need the loving help and support from other Christians to grow and develop in faith and ability. Since the world is comprised of sinners, we certainly can't be too bad to attend and be involved in church.

If we want to be Christians, we should be attending church on a regular basis because it is not complete without us. When we are missing, some mission of the church is not fulfilled. We have so many blessings from God, it is only right we share them with others. What better place to do that than in his church?

Looking around us, what signs have we seen that can inspire us to become the Christians God wants us to be? What nourishment from the church and fellow Christians can we use to improve our attitudes and actions? The best time to start is now by following yet another church sign: *come in and have your faith lifted*.

Come and Journey With Me

Music and Text by David Haas

Come to the song, come to the dance.
Bring all you are, bring all you'd be;
And come with your voice, come with your heart.
Come and journey with me.
Come and journey with me.

Come, let the sun fill up your eyes,
Take the time to look around,
And love, just love; and walk with each other.
Come and journey with me.
Come and journey with me.

Come and see, come and be,
Be all you are, and all you can be;
And leave all behind, and calm your mind.
Come and journey with me.
Come and journey with me.

God is taking each of us on a fabulous journey. It is full of twists and turns, highs and lows, triumphs and failures, change and growth. But mostly it is a journey of love. God loves us as if there was only one of us in all the world. His infinite love bathes us in support and encouragement because God only seeks the best for us.

What do we need to do in return? We need to seek God and follow His will to the best of our abilities. And God has promised to be with us every step of the way. The Lord is good to those whose hope is in him, to the one who seeks him. Lamentations 3:25

The Devil's Tools for Sale

It was advertised that the devil was going to put his tools up for sale. Once the date of the sale of the tools were placed for public inspection, each was marked with its sale price. They were a treacherous lot of implements. Hatred, Envy, Jealousy, Deceit, Lying, Pride, and so on, comprised the outfit. Laid apart from the rest was a harmless-looking tool, well-worn, and priced very high.

"What is the name of this tool?" asked one of the purchasers, pointing to it.

"That is Discouragement," tersely replied the devil.

"Why have you priced it so high?"

"Because it is more useful to me than the others. I can pry open and get inside a person's heart with that when I cannot get near them with other tools. Once I get inside, I can make that person do what I choose. The tool is badly worn because I use it on almost everyone, since few people know it belongs to me."
Author Unknown

What tools should we use instead of the devil's crafty and sinister ones? Saint Paul reminds us that our tools should involve love. He describes love in this way:

Love is patient, love is kind. It is not jealous, (love) is not pompous, it is not inflated, it is not rude, it does not seek its own interests, it is not quick-tempered, it does not brood over injury, it does not rejoice over wrongdoing but rejoices with the truth. It bears all things, believes all things, hopes all things, endures all things. Love never fails. If there are prophecies, they will be brought to nothing; if tongues, they will cease; if knowledge, it will be brought to nothing. For we know partially and we prophesy partially, but when the perfect comes, the partial will pass away. When I was a child, I used to talk as a child, think as a child, reason as a child; when I became a man, I put aside childish things. At present we see indistinctly, as in a mirror, but then face to face. At present I know partially; then I shall know fully, as I am fully known. So faith, hope, love remain, these three; but the greatest of these is love. 1 Corinthians 13:4–13

These tools are just the opposite of what the devil uses on us.

Whenever in our daily lives we come in contact with the devil's evil tool of discouragement we should seek God's help and guidance. *I command you: be firm and steadfast (have courage)! Do not fear nor be dismayed, for the Lord, your God, is with you wherever you go. Joshua 1:9*

The Psalmist states our situation very well.

We are afflicted in every way, but not constrained; perplexed, but not driven to despair; persecuted, but not abandoned; struck down, but not destroyed; always carrying about in the body the dying of Jesus, so that the life of Jesus may also be manifested in our body. For we who live are constantly being given up to death for the sake of Jesus, so that the life of Jesus may be manifested in our mortal flesh.

So death is at work in us, but life in you. Since, then, we have the same spirit of faith, according to what is written, "I believed, therefore I spoke," we too believe and therefore speak, knowing that the one who raised the Lord Jesus will raise us also with Jesus and place us with you in his presence. Everything indeed is for you, so that the grace bestowed in abundance on more and more people may cause the thanksgiving to overflow for the glory of God. Therefore, we are not discouraged; rather, although our outer self is wasting away, our inner self is being renewed day by day. For this momentary light affliction is producing for us an eternal weight of glory beyond all comparison, as we look not to what is seen but to what is unseen; for what is seen is transitory, but what is unseen is eternal. 2 Corinthians 4:8–18

When discouragement hits, **"Put on the armor of God so that you may be able to stand firm against the tactics of the devil." Ephesians 6:11**

Remember what the Psalmist says:

"Your word, Lord, stands forever; it is firm as the heavens. I am yours; save me, for I cherish your precepts." Psalm 119:89, 94

If we diligently read and follow the Lord's words we will never have to fret or have concern about any of the tools the devil has for sale.

Do List

We are familiar with the don'ts in our life. Don't talk back. Don't think evil thoughts of others. Don't plan revenge on someone who did something to you that you didn't like or think you deserved. Our parents, as well as our community and church, have given us many don'ts to follow. We need don'ts in our life. But we also need to concentrate on the dos and shoulds.

We should love our neighbors as ourselves. We must treat them with kindness and gentleness as we would treat Christ himself.

Do you repay unkindness with gentleness and prayer? Do you pray for those who treat you badly? Do you provide help and guidance to those who need it? Do you invite others to join you at church? At play? At times of celebration?

Take time to look at possibilities to do random acts of kindness and perform senseless acts of beauty. Look what you can do to spread God's kingdom. Discover what you can do to be more like Jesus. Follow the Nike commercial and "just do it." Think positively. Be positive. And do positive things with the life God has given you.

Dear children, let us not love with words or tongue but with actions and in truth. 1 John 3:18

Dear friends, let us love one another, for love comes from God. Everyone who loves has been born of God and knows God. Whoever does not love does not know God, because God is love. 1 John 4:7, 8

Dear friends, since God so loved us, we also ought to love one another. 1 John 4:11

Therefore, as God's chosen people, holy and dearly loved, clothe yourselves with compassion, kindness, humility, gentleness and patience. Bear with each other and forgive whatever grievances you may have against one another. Forgive as the Lord forgave you. Colossians 3:12, 13

Love must be sincere. Hate what is evil; cling to what is good. Be devoted to one another in brotherly love. Honor one another above yourselves. Romans 12:9, 10

Don't Worry; Be Happy

As long as the future is in the loving hands of God, we don't have to worry about it. For even though we may not know what our future holds, we do know who holds it.

This quote from one of the pastors who contributed to the devotional book Meditations, 2012, reminds us that all of our life, all of our problems, all of our needs are in the hands of God. That's better than Allstate any day. That's better than State Farm Insurance or any other business that claims to take worry out of our hands and put it into theirs. God is constant. God is powerful. And above all God is loving. God will keep us safe in his arms.

Will we have problems? Yes. Will we have decisions to make? Yes. Will we have to live with our actions? Yes. But praying to God for guidance and then accepting the response allows us to reduce our worries and concerns. Being human, we probably will never be able to rid ourselves of worry completely, but we can reduce it immeasurably by trusting in God and knowing that he has our best interests in mind. Once our choice is made, we ask God for help in living with and enjoying the decision.

We need to trust in God, make a decision after having prayerfully thought about it, and then accept the consequences he has set out for us. Do not worry about the future. God has already seen it and knows what is best for us. He has carved us in the palm of his hand, and we can't ask for any better security than that.

Can a mother forget the baby at her breast and have no compassion on the child she has borne? Though she may forget, I will not forget you! Isaiah 49:15, 16

Everyday Love

Are you an ordinary person? Of course you are. So what? Everyday people can show their love for the Lord as well as the heroes and champions of old have done. Really!

The trick is to put your love for God into your daily life. That may be giving hugs to small children and even "large" children when they need it. It doesn't seem heroic, but it is.

How about the times you celebrated the joys of others even when you were hurting? That's heroic. It isn't flashy or newsworthy, but it is momentous.

Your love may be expressed in the form of understanding and support for others who are having difficulties. Those people certainly appreciate your efforts. These efforts are one of many endless possibilities of being magnanimous to people.

Forgiveness is also a heroic act. Seek forgiveness from others, extend your forgiveness to those you meet, and seek forgiveness from God when you slip into sin. We are Christians when we show our love to others by pardoning them.

Just because we haven't saved a nation from destruction or created a large charitable organization or completed some massive task doesn't mean we can't show our heroic love for God and others in our ordinary lives. It's all a matter of commitment to love in our own circumstances in life. We all can do that.

Let the morning bring me word of your unfailing love, for I have put my trust in you. Show me the way I should go, for to you I lift up my soul. Psalm 143:8

For your love is ever before me, and I walk continually in your truth. Psalm 26:3

Every Star in the Sky

Every star in the sky should remind us of God's love which is powerful, vast, never-ending and breath-taking.

Thank God for a caterpillar becoming a butterfly, parents loving their children, the Grand Canyon, waterfalls, the four seasons, the joy of a wedding, and the solar system.

God is bigger and more powerful than anything we can think of in our minds or feel with our hearts. He is more complex than any of the items listed above. The things God can do, has done, and will do in the future are more numerous than the stars in the sky.

If that is the case, why do we ever feel lonely or abandoned? Of all of God's creations, none are more important than us. His son died for us. Jesus rose from the dead for us. All of creation is only a prelude to what is in store for us in heaven. Armed with this knowledge, never let yourself feel lonely, abandoned, or without hope again.

There is no fear in love. But perfect love drives out fear, because fear has to do with punishment. The one who fears is not yet made perfect in love. I John 4:18

If you make the Most High your dwelling—even the Lord, who is my refuge— then no harm will befall you, no disaster will come near your tent. For he will command his angels concerning you to guard you in all your ways; they will lift you up in their hands, so that you will not strike your foot against a stone. Psalm 91:9–12

Have no fear of sudden disaster or of the ruin that overtakes the wicked, for the Lord will be your confidence and will keep your foot from being snared. Proverbs 3:25, 26

For God did not give us a spirit of timidity, but a spirit of power, of love and of self-discipline. 2 Timothy 1:7

Exercise Daily—Walk With the Lord!

In a jungle, your eyes, ears, and nose are bombarded with scents, colors, and sounds. It is a fantastic place to walk, appreciate nature, and ponder the meaning of life. The breathtaking experience would continue to reverberate in your mind for many years.

Besides the benefits of the experience, you would be exercising. Exercise is helpful to your heart, lungs, and respiratory system. You would obtain many benefits with minimal effort.

The benefits of being in a jungle on your body are nothing compared to the rewards of being with God. Walking with God would certainly stimulate your senses. It would invigorate your life by changing your attitudes and making you aware of the wonders God has in store for you.

Strolling with God will stimulate blood flow. Really! Your heart will expand its capacity to love and be loved. You will take in wonders you have never seen before. People and events will embody new meaning and importance. Life will become fuller.

Your improved heart will encourage you to improve your lungs. You will take in God's word, hear God's voice, and drink in God's sacraments.

You will inhale freely and exhale many impurities you so jealously held on to before.

Your circulatory system will not be left behind. You will find new energy to complete tasks, encourage people in difficulty, look for the bright side of injuries or illness, and you will fill up your time with essential things in life. Your priorities will help you to accomplish more with the same amount of time as you had before.

Sound impossible? Not with God. He loves you so dearly he will support you and encourage you in all your endeavors. Your part is to walk with God, be his friend, and allow him to become the most important part of your life. Exercise, anyone?

The Lord your God is with you, he is mighty to save. He will take great delight in you, he will quiet you with his love, he will rejoice over you with singing."
Zephaniah 3:17

Faith, Work, and Heaven

For the kingdom of heaven is like a landowner who went out early in the morn-ing to hire men to work in his vineyard. He agreed to pay them a denarius for the day and sent them into his vineyard.

About the third hour he went out and saw others standing in the marketplace doing nothing. He told them, "You also go and work in my vineyard, and I will pay you whatever is right so they went. He went out again about the sixth hour and the ninth hour and did the same thing.

About the eleventh hour he went out and found still others standing around. He asked them, "Why have you been standing here all day long doing noth-ing?" "Because no one has hired us, "they answered. He said to them, "You also go and work in my vineyard."

When evening came, the owner of the vineyard said to his foreman, "Call the workers and pay them their wages, beginning with the last ones hired and go-ing on to the first."

The workers who were hired about the eleventh hour came and each received a denarius. So when those came who were hired first, they expected to receive more. But each one of them also received a denarius. When they received it, they began to grumble against the landowner. "These men who were hired last worked only one hour," they said, "and you have made them equal to us who have borne the burden of the work and the heat of the day."

But he answered one of them, "Friend, I am not being unfair to you. Didn't you agree to work for a denarius? Take your pay and go. I want to give the man who was hired last the same as I gave you. Don't I have the right to do what I want with my own money? Or are you envious because I am generous?" So the last will be first, and the first will be last. Matthew 20:1

Many of us have never liked the above reading. It seems to go against our sense of fair play. The men who worked one hour were treated just like the ones who worked the entire day. Is that fair?

But if we think of the situation in terms of salvation, maybe we would feel differently. Suppose the workers who toiled the entire day are those people who have faith in God and never waver throughout their whole life. The reward is heaven (one denarius). We know we have been working for God and expect a just ending to our faith and work. Now suppose the ones who worked the last hour are those people who have not believed in the Savior. They have, throughout their life, done what they pleased and did not worry about what God wants them to do. Then, in the last hour, they have a change of heart (Metanoia) and decide to diligently work for the Lord. Shouldn't they receive a just reward (heaven)? Of course of they should. The fact that they believed in Jesus and his message of salvation so late in their life does not negate their chance to earn eternal life. Thank God! That means there is always hope for salvation.

Would we, as lifelong believers, like to gamble at losing heaven? Would we like to take the chance that we might finally believe in God in the last hour of the day after having spent the rest of the day as an unbeliever? Since we know not the day nor the hour of our death, it is comforting to realize we are believers and will go to Heaven. We don't have to worry about the day or the hour because we know our Lord will gladly accept us into his kingdom. Working all day for the Lord is not easy, but it is reassuring. It is not a disadvantage to have spent our time in service of God because we are confident in the result of that faith and service.

For the wages of sin is death, but the gift of God is eternal life in Christ Jesus our Lord. Romans 6:23

I have not come to call the righteous, but sinners to repentance. Luke 5:32

He said to them, "Go into all the world and preach the good news to all creation. Whoever believes and is baptized will be saved, but whoever does not believe will be condemned." Mark 16:15, 16

For God so loved the world that he gave his one and only son, that whoever believes in him shall not perish but have eternal life. John 3:16

First Class

There is the joke of the dumb blonde getting on a plane and sitting in the first class section. When a man came to sit in her seat he asked to see her ticket. He informed her that she had a third-class ticket and would have to move. She looked at the man and stated, "I'm blonde and beautiful, and I'm going to New York." Frustrated by his attempt to convince the blonde of her error, he called on the flight attendant for help.

The flight attendant asked to see the woman's ticket. He then told her she had a third-class seat and should move to that section. She looked at the flight attendant and announced, "I'm blonde and beautiful and am going to New York." Seeing they were getting nowhere with the woman, they called on the captain.

The captain looked at the blonde's ticket and agreed that indeed it was a third-class ticket and she would have to move. The blonde again stated, "I'm blonde and beautiful and am going to New York."

The captain then whispered into the woman's ear. She responded, "Why didn't anyone tell me this before?" She immediately got up and went to the third-class section.

Amazed, the flight attendant and first class passenger asked the captain what he had told the blonde. He informed them that he just told her first class doesn't stop in New York.

Whether you think the joke is funny or not, you can draw a lesson from it. When I think about this joke, I view plane as my life. I am bound for heaven and not New York. The captain is God. Unlike the passenger in the joke, God wants all of us in first class. None of us deserve to be in second or third class. The devil is always trying to convince us that first class is not where we belong and heaven is not our destination. We need to remember that our ticket has been paid for by the birth, death, and resurrection of Jesus Christ and that we are all first-class passengers in the eyes of God. We are never dumb blonds related to a lower class seat.

When Jesus spoke again to the people, he said, "I am the light of the world. Whoever follows me will never walk in darkness, but will have the light of life." John 8:12

The Lord is my light and my salvation—whom shall I fear? The Lord is the stronghold of my life—of whom shall I be afraid? Psalm 27:1

For God so loved the world that he gave his one and only Son, that whoever believes in him shall not perish but have eternal life John 3:16

Forgive Yourself

We have all heard the expression "Don't cry over spilt milk." We obviously couldn't pick up the spilt milk in a useful way. But so often we do worry about past mistakes as if they were spilt milk. We feel guilt for the bad things we have done. Guilt is a waste of time and doesn't lead to improvement or action. Linda Allison-Lewis states that we should "Forgive [ourselves] in an instant. God does!" What a wonderful idea. God has already pardoned us, so why should we not forgive ourselves? When it comes to sin, we should ask for forgiveness from God, learn from our error, forgive ourselves, and then move on. Don't waste time with guilt. We should seek God's help to learn from our mistake then resolve to improve. Forgive, forget, and move on.

We still have to worry about the consequences of our sins and we will still have to deal with those results. If we have injured another person, it may be difficult to associate with them because they haven't forgiven us. They may have confided about their dislike for us to other people, which leads those people to deal harshly with us. It will be difficult to interact with those people kindly or react gently if they resent us and show us their resentment and anger in words and by their actions. The sin is gone, but the consequences remain. It will take all our prayers and strength to act Christ-like in our daily dealings with people we have hurt and we can't allow guilt add any additional weight to our burdens.

God has given up his son to death for our sins, past, present, and future. Since God has already absolved our sins, we need to forgive ourselves. With God's help we can forget our past sins, and then grow in wisdom and love in service of God in the future. It all starts with forgiveness.

As far as the east is from the west, so far has he removed our transgressions from us. Psalm 103:12

You forgave the iniquity of your people and covered all their sins. Psalm 85:2

For I will forgive their wickedness and will remember their sins no more. Hebrews 8:12

My dear children, I write this to you so that you will not sin. But if anybody does sin, we have one who speaks to the Father in our defense—Jesus Christ, the Righteous One. 1 John 2:1

For the Honor and Glory of God

I am so angry. That guy just cut me off in this heavy traffic. I hope he gets a flat tire and people just pass him by without so much as a thought of helping him. I wish this would happen for the honor and glory of God.

I just donated some very used clothing to St. Vincent de Paul. But its' good enough for people who can't afford quality clothes. Maybe if they worked as hard as I did, they wouldn't be in such tough shape. A little work wouldn't hurt them. I also claimed as much as possible for tax purposes, even though the clothes are not worth that much. I will do this for the honor and glory of God.

The neighbor's kids are such losers. They leave their bikes all over the place. Such a hazard! Someone could get hurt if they are carrying groceries into the house and they don't see the bikes. Maybe if I ran over a bike or hid them for a week, it would teach the kids a lesson. I will do this for the honor and glory of God.

Hopefully these examples of our possible actions are very jarring to our senses. Our decisions might be quite different if we always said and thought that what we were doing was for the honor and glory of God.

If we always did things consciously for the honor and glory of God, would we be more kind? Would we be more considerate of others and their feelings? Would our judgments change if we realized that God is present with us all the time? Would our anger be abated? Would our cursing cease? Would our outbursts be stifled?

God does not expect us to be perfect and doesn't condemn us for our failings. But he does expect us to pray to him for assistance and guidance in overcoming our weaknesses. He wants us to love our neighbors as ourselves and to treat them accordingly. God does plan for reformation and transformation in our ability to relate lovingly to others.

That means we need to be humble, pray, and be open to God's many graces that will enable us to grow and change so that what we do and think in the future will actually be done for the honor and glory of God.

I urge you, brothers, in view of God's mercy, to offer your bodies as living sacrifices, holy and pleasing to God—this is your spiritual act of worship. Romans 12:1

Through Jesus…let us continually offer to God a sacrifice of praise—the fruit of lips that confess his name. And do not forget to do good and to share with others, for with such sacrifice God is pleased. Hebrews 13:15–16

To do what is right and just is more acceptable to the Lord than sacrifice. Proverbs 21:3

And just as you want men to treat you, treat them in the same way. Luke 6:31

This is my commandment, that you love one another, as I have loved you. Greater love has no man than this, that a man lay down his life for his friends. John 15:12–13

If our hearts do not condemn us, we have confidence before God and receive from him anything we ask, because we obey his commands and do what pleases him. And this his command: to believe in the name of his son, Jesus Christ, and to love one another as he commanded us. 1 John 3:21–23

Dear Heavenly Father,

You have given me love that is beyond human understanding, and I am your loving servant. May the love that I feel for you be reflected in the compassion that I show to my family, to my friends, and to all who cross my path. Amen

Prayer taken from *Friend, Promises, Praises and Prayers.* Published by Family Christian Press 2003.

Fresh Start

Then I acknowledged my sin to you and did not cover up my iniquity. I said, "I will confess my transgressions to the Lord"—and you forgave the guilt of my sin. Psalm 32:5

"Oops! I goofed again. I'll never get this right. I am such a loser." It is a reassuring thing to know that God doesn't believe us or accept our faults as reason not to love us. Our faults aren't allowed to stop us from achieving what God wants us to achieve. He overrides any of our faults with his grace, faith, and encouragement.

So what do we do when we feel inadequate? What do we do when we have failed time after time? What do we do when we are discouraged and ready to give up?

The answer is to believe in God, get up, and try again. Like the sun, we need to see each new day as a new beginning, a fresh start. The sun doesn't reflect on the wrongs of yesterday but brightly shines (even when behind clouds) on the events to come. It neither feels bad nor accepts past failures. It begins each new sunrise with a fresh start.

Unlike the sun we do have feelings. We do get discouraged, make mistakes, and have to accept the consequences of our actions. God loves us and wants us to start over after our failures. He will provide us with what we need to overcome our inadequacies. God has forgotten our sins and has provided us with many opportunities to begin again. He will continue to give that support and encouragement in the future, too. So relax. God is in control and will always be there whenever we require his assistance.

I will give you a new heart and put a new spirit in you; I will remove from you your heart of stone and give you a heart of flesh. Ezekiel 36:26

Frog Love?

We have all heard variations of the story of the little boy named Tom and his pet frog. The boy took care of the frog. The frog went everywhere he went. Much attention and care was devoted to his frog.

One day his older brother, Jim, asked him how much he liked his frog.

"Oh, I love my frog," said Tom "I take care of it, feed it, and have made a home for it in the back yard using my own money. I love this frog more than anything in the world. I wouldn't ever let anything bad happen to my frog."

Jim asked, "Do you love your frog enough to become a frog yourself?"

"Well, no," responded Tom. "I guess I don't love my frog that much. But I do like him a lot."

Adapted from a true experience from Fr. Mike Martinez

"Love" is a word we use quite frequently and probably without much thought. We don't prioritize our feelings toward our friends, our relatives, our possessions and God. We "love" them all. Maybe we need to rethink that concept. Maybe we only like certain things, but really don't love them.

"For God so loved the world that he gave his one and only son, that whoever believes in him shall not perish but have eternal life. For God did not send his son into the world to condemn the world, but to save the world through him. Whoever believes in him is not condemned, but whoever does not believe stands condemned already because he has not believed in the name of God's one and only son. This is the verdict: Light has come into the world, but men loved darkness instead of light because their deeds were evil. Everyone who does evil hates the light, and will not come into the light for fear that his deeds will be exposed. But whoever lives by the truth comes into the light, so that it may be seen plainly that what he has done has been done through God." John 3:16–21

God loved us so much he chose to become a "frog," just like us. He was willing to humble himself and take on the hopes, fears, and troubles of humanity. That is real love, not just caring. Real love involves complete commitment, not just superficial pronouncements.

Do we like God enough to attend church on a regular basis? Or do we love God enough that what we hear and learn in church is used to change our lives?

Do we like God enough to avoid dealing with people we don't appreciate? Or do we love God enough that we forgive those we don't like and pray for them?

Do we like God enough that we profess to other church members our good intentions of helping others with time and money? Or do we love God enough that we become involved with the less fortunate and even open ourselves up to share their pain and suffering, to become actively involved in their lives, their hopes, fears, and ideas?

Do we like God enough to work on dealing with our friends and relatives' concerns? Or do we love God enough that we sacrifice our comfort to support our friends and family? Have we put out as much effort we possibly can to alleviate their suffering? Have we unselfishly given of our time even at the cost of our own freedom? Are our choices based on love of God or interest in ourselves?

The list of "likes" in our lives is enormous. It could span several notebooks with small spaced lines. Our God, on the other hand is asking us to love, to put the needs of others in front of our own needs. We are to extend and stretch ourselves to the service and benefit of others, all in God's name. We are to show his love for humankind by our actions. In other words, we are to practice what we learn and preach. We are to love others, just like God, who sent his only son to become a human, just like us.

We should start today to look at our ideas, patterns, and actions to see how loving they are. We should peer into our lives and see where we can change from "liking" to "loving," and when and where we can begin to make those changes. It is easy to like the "frogs" in our lives, but it's quite another to love, cherish and demonstrate our love for them.

"Love the Lord your God with all your heart and with all your soul and with all your mind and with all your strength." The second is this: "Love your neighbor as yourself." There is no commandment greater than these. To love him with all your heart, with all your understanding and with all your strength, and to love your neighbor as yourself is more important than all burnt offerings and sacrifices." Mark 12:30, 31, 33

My command is this: Love each other as I have loved you. Greater love has no one than this, that he lay down his life for his friends. You are my friends if you do what I command. This is my command: Love each other. Mark 12:30, 31, 33

And so we know and rely on the love God has for us. God is love. Whoever lives in love lives in God, and God in him. And he has given us this command: Whoever loves God must also love his brother. 1 John 4:16, 21

.

Fruit

I hope these fruit messages will remind you that the body and soul both need nutrition daily to be healthy.

Watermelon is sweet and juicy. So are God's words and his sacraments.

Life can be "peachy." It takes prayers said daily to accomplish.

Kiwi is an exotic fruit for Americans. Your communion with God shouldn't be that way. It should be the most ordinary thing you do each day.

An apple a day keeps the doctor away. Constant prayer keeps the devil away.

"Orange" you glad you know God? Read all about him in your Bible

Whatever God says to us is full of living power: it is sharper than the sharpest dagger, cutting swift and deep into our innermost thoughts and desires with all their parts, exposing us for what we really are. Hebrews 4:12

But the fruit of the Spirit is love, joy, peace, patience, kindness, goodness, faithfulness, gentleness and self-control. Galatians 5:22–23

God Can Use Us

But you are a chosen people, a royal priesthood, a holy nation, a people be-longing to God, that you may declare the praises of him who called you out of darkness into his wonderful light. 1 Peter 2:9

But I am not worthy. I don't know what to do. I am not able to express myself as well as others. I am too shy. What if I make a mistake?

Although we have been anointed by our baptism as priest, prophet, and king, we really don't believe it. Doubt about our abilities to profess our faith to others is always a fear we have to overcome. We have to rely on God to do the work. By ourselves we certainly will do a inadequate job. But with God's support, something he has promised us, we can be a wit-ness to our faith.

If we look back at Jonah, we can see God's power and authority. Jonah ran away from God's call to go to Niveveh and tell them to repent. Jonah felt unworthy and felt he would be of better use someplace else. God had different plans for Jonah. He created a storm that threatened to destroy the boat Jonah was on. Jonah convinced the Phoenecian sailors on the boat that it was his fault God created the storm and pleaded with the Phoenecians to throw him overboard. Once that was done, the storm died down as quickly as it had occurred. By this miracle the Phoenecians believed in the one true God. They realized this God of the Jews was much more powerful and real than their own gods. They had been wit-nessed to by Jonah in a way he never imagined. He helped convert the men by his lack of faith in God. God turned that lack of faith into an action that caused others to accept God as God. Even in Jonah's lack of faith, his bungling of the situation, something fantastic came from the situation: conversion of the Phoenecians.

The lesson we learn is that God will work through us no matter how incapable and inarticulate we feel we are. God is in control and will do the work. We just have to be willing to serve and to be open to God's power. Yes, we are weak. Yes, we are not adequate by ourselves. But God will use our abilities and lack of abilities to accomplish much good. If he can compel a runaway prophet to evangelize, then there is hope for us too in our own stumbling and even reluctant efforts to witness our faith.

And my God will meet all your needs according to his glorious riches in Christ Jesus. Philippians 4:19

In God I trust; I will not be afraid. What can man do to me? Psalm 56:11

God Does Not Call the Equipped. He Equips the Called

I know what it is to be in need, and I know what it is to have plenty. I have learned the secret of being content in any and every situation, whether well fed or hungry, whether living in plenty or in want. I can do everything through him who gives me strength. Philippians 4:12, 13

God calls each one of us for his purpose. We alone can accomplish his plan for us. Do not fear. Do not doubt. Do not be tepid. God has promised us he will provide whatever we require. All we must to do is give our best efforts in whatever we do.

God will channel us, motivate us and equip us with the knowledge, tools and people essential in our quest to do his will. Our faith in him along with our prayers and petitions will be all that we need to be successful. God will not call us unless he sufficiently equips us to do the job.

Have I not commanded you? Be strong and courageous. Do not be terrified; do not be discouraged, for the Lord your God will be with you wherever you go. Joshua 1:9

Know therefore that the Lord is God; he is the faithful God, keeping his covenant of love to a thousand generations of those who love him and keep his commands. Deuteronomy 7:9

Ask and it will be given to you; seek and you will find; knock and the door will be opened to you. For everyone who asks, receives; and the one who seeks, finds; and to the one who knocks, the door will be opened. Which one of you would hand his son a stone when he asks for a loaf of bread, or a snake when he asks for a fish? If you then, who are wicked, know how to give good gifts to your children, how much more will your heavenly Father give good things to those who ask him. Matthew 7:7–12

God is Like an Old Commercial

God is like Bayer Aspirin. He works wonders.
God is like Dial soap. Aren't you glad you know him?
Don't you wish everybody did?
God is like Sears. He has everything.
God is like Scotch tape. You can't see him, but you know he's there.

We, as humans, have the need to organize things and put them into neat little boxes or concepts in order to understand and accept them. The more we can visualize something or put it into a category, the better we can use the concept in our daily lives. We even do that with God. We put him into a petite box so we can describe him to others and ourselves and feel comfortable with the idea of him. But God is much more than anything we can describe, feel, conceptualize or understand. We need to accept the fact we will never be able to wholly understand God and all that he represents. Because of faith, we accept God, attempt to learn as much as we can about him, and try to use his ideas about how we should live our lives as shown to us by his son, Jesus Christ.

We should continue to describe God as best we can and realize he is much more complex and magnificent than anything we can picture of him. Still, the more we know God, the more essential he becomes in our lives. The more important he becomes in our lives, the better opportunity we will have to be transformed into the person he intends for us to become. Our lives will be more joyous and complete. It is a never-ending process, one that will cease only when we die and enter our heavenly home to encounter God face to face.

Listed below are some more commercials and scripture readings that help to describe our Lord.

God is like Coke. He's the real thing.

For God so loved the world that he gave his only son, so that everyone who believes in him might not perish but might have eternal life. John 3:16

God is like Pam Am. He makes the going great.

He said: I love you, Lord, my strength, Lord, my rock, my fortress, my deliverer, my God, my rock of refuge, my shield, my saving horn, my stronghold! Psalm 18:2, 3

God is like Tide. He gets the stains out that others leave behind.

But God, who is rich in mercy, because of the great love he had for us, even when we were dead in our transgressions, brought us to life with Christ (by grace you have been saved), raised us up with him, and seated us with him in the heavens in Christ Jesus, that in the ages to come he might show the immeasurable riches of his grace in his kindness to us in Christ Jesus. For by grace you have been saved through faith, and this is not from you; it is the gift of God; it is not from works, so no one may boast. For we are his handiwork, created in Christ Jesus for the good works that God has prepared in advance, that we should live in them. Ephesians 2:8–10.

God is like VO5 hairspray. He holds through all kinds of weather.

Though the mountains leave their place and the hills be shaken, My love shall never leave you nor my covenant of peace be shaken, says the Lord, who has mercy on you. Isaiah 54:10

God is like General Electric. He lights your path.

In all your ways be mindful of him, and he will make straight your paths. Be not wise in your own eyes, fear the Lord and turn away from evil; this will mean health for your flesh and vigor for your bones. Honor the Lord with your wealth, with first fruits of all your produce; then will your barns be filled with grain, with new wine your vats will overflow. The discipline of the Lord, my son, disdain not; spurn not his reproof; for whom the Lord loves he reproves, and he chastises the son he favors. Proverbs 3:6–12

God is like Hallmark cards. He cares enough to send the very best.

And I will ask the father, and he will give you another Advocate to be with you always, the Spirit of truth, which the world cannot accept, because it neither sees nor knows it. But you know it, because it remains with you, and will be in you. I will not leave you orphans; I will come to you. In a little while the world will no longer see me, but you will see me, because I live and you will live. On that day you will realize that I am in my Father and you are in me and I in you. Whoever has my commandments and observes them is the one who loves me. And whoever loves me will be loved by my father, and I will love him and reveal myself to him." John 10:16–21

God is eager and able to support and guide us in our struggle to uncover more about him and ourselves. We must be open to God's messages like the scripture reading below given to the ancient Israelites but meant for all of us.

"And now, Israel, what does the Lord, your God, ask of you but to fear the Lord, your God, and follow his ways exactly, to love and serve the Lord, your God, with all your heart and all your soul, to keep the commandments and statutes of the Lord which I enjoin on you today for your own good?

Think! The heavens, even the highest heavens, belong to the Lord, your God, as well as the earth and everything on it. Yet in his love for your fathers the

Lord was so attached to them as to choose you, their descendants, in prefer-
ence to all other peoples, as indeed he has now done.

Circumcise your hearts, therefore, and be no longer stiff-necked. For the Lord,
your God, is the God of gods, the Lord of lords, the great God, mighty and
awesome, who has no favorites, accepts no bribes; who executes justice for the
orphan and the widow, and befriends the alien, feeding and clothing him. So
you too must befriend the alien, for you were once aliens yourselves in the land
of Egypt.

The Lord, your God, shall you fear, and him shall you serve; hold fast to him
and swear by his name. He is your glory, he, your God, who has done for you
those great and terrible things which your own eyes have seen. Your ancestors
went down to Egypt seventy strong, and now the Lord, your God, has made
you as numerous as the stars of the sky. Deuteronomy 10:12–22

As we continue the process of learning more about God, let us praise his
holy name.

Shout joyfully to the Lord, all you lands; worship the Lord with cries of glad-
ness; come before him with joyful song. Know that the Lord is God, our maker
to whom we belong, whose people we are, God's well-tended flock. Enter the
temple gates with praise, its courts with thanksgiving. Give thanks to God,
bless his name; good indeed is the Lord, Whose love endures forever, whose
faithfulness lasts through every age. Psalm 100:1-5

God Is Like #2

God is like Coke. He's the real thing.

God is like Pam Am. He makes the going great.

God is like General Electric. He lights your path.

God is like Bayer Aspirin. He works wonders.

God is like Hallmark Cards. He cares enough to send the very best.

God is like Tide. He gets the stains out that others leave behind.

God is like VO5 hairspray. He holds through all kinds of weather.

God is like Dial Soap. Aren't you glad you know him? Don't you wish everybody did?

God is like Sears. He has everything.

God is like Alka Seltzer. Try him. You'll like him.

God is like Scotch tape. You can't see him but you know he's there.

New Commercials

God is like Ace. He's the helpful place.

God is like AVIS. He's number one.

God is like Enterprise. He will pick you up.

God is like Fry's. He's the savings place.

God is like Motel 6. He'll leave the light on for you.

God is like Wheaties. He's the breakfast of champions.

These commercials are catchy. They are short reminders of what the product has to offer. They encourage us to use them to make our lives easier or better. They can be had for a limited amount of money.

God provides us with the means to a worthwhile earthly life and an opportunity to obtain eternal life in heaven. He lifts us, encourages us, nourishes us, and gives us every human necessity if only we believe in him and follow his commandments. That is far better than the temporary relief any of these products in the commercials can offer us.

Spend some time on things that will last, on the peace and serenity only God can provide. Spend time with God, getting to know him on an intimate level. Spend time being nourished by his word and sacraments. In other words, use your time wisely, letting God be involved with all aspects of your life. Let him be the "real commercial" in solving and dealing with the struggles and challenges in your daily life. As Speedy Alka Seltzer would say, "Try him. You'll like him."

And God is able to make all grace abound toward you; that you, always having all sufficiency in all things, may abound to every good work. 2 Corinthians 9:8

God Whispers

God often whispers in our hearts and speaks quietly to our soul. Too often in life we don't hear the quiet voice but need to have someone throw a brick at us to get our attention. (Paraphrased from quote on the internet)

We have all heard stories or seen TV movies where someone has a heart attack. After the serious situation, the person makes major changes in their life. We also find out that there were warning signs before the catastrophe. The person disregarded the little warnings but could not ignore the heart attack.

God is like that. He often provides us with insights and reminders of what to do. It may be the suggestion from your child you should attend church. It could be your neighbor inviting you to serve at a soup kitchen. The pastor could even be coaxing you into some ministry at your church. All those earthy ideas may be God, incognito, hinting to us how he would like us to energize and reorganize our lives.

Our job is to be open to suggestions and pray for guidance. Reviewing what has happened in our day and looking for God's gentle whisper is important too. These methods can help us be ready when God whispers to us. Don't wait for a heart attack, accident, or illness to make us aware of what we should be doing. Listen to God's coaxing and do not expect his revelations to be in some dramatic force like fireworks or a tornado. God whispers gently to us through his word, church, and people. Listen and be ready to respond.

So Eli told Samuel, "Go and lie down, and if he calls you, say, 'Speak, Lord, for your servant is listening.'" So Samuel went and lay down in his place. The Lord came and stood there, calling as at the other times, "Samuel! Samuel!" Then Samuel said, "Speak, for your servant is listening." 1 Samuel 3:9, 10

Goodness

It has been sung in song and read in verse that the earth if full of the goodness of God. Do we really believe this? Are we sure the earth is full of virtue and pleasantness? What about all the horrible things that happen in this world? It is true that evil and sin are in the world and others who sin have an effect on us. And it is also accurate to understand that terrible things happen to terrific people.

So where is the goodness? It's everywhere! All we need to do is know how and where to look. Have you seen the most beautiful sunrise or sunset lately? It brings joy to the heart and is a vision to behold. But we must find the time and the interest to notice it. If we don't see it, it is not because it isn't there, but rather that we missed the opportunity to notice it. God generously provides many opportunities to see the handiwork of his magnificent hands, but too often we are too preoccupied to appreciate it. We need to make for the effort to soak in the multitude of blessings surrounding us.

Have you pondered the fact little children are happy with items and situations we take for granted? They smile at tickles and attention shown to them by adults. They are in awe of the wonder of butterflies, flowers, and a host of common, ordinary events. It is all so simple, but we have forgotten how much pleasure those uncomplicated situations can bring to our mind and body.

Is there ever any more abundance of color than watching the leaves in fall turn to rich hues of red, brown, and yellow? Have you taken a drive to a hill to observe the splendor? What about the brilliant panoramic view of a lake or the ocean? How about the majestic mountain near your home? How about the explosion of color and fragrance when flowers bloom in springtime? You have the gas and the mode of transportation but do you bother to turn on the engine and leave the remote control on the couch?

We probably forget how wonderful it is to just be with our close friends. They make us laugh, cry, sing, and dance. Why not engineer more quality time to enjoy their company? It may difficult to arrange schedules to accommodate this, but it is worth it.

Have you been associating consistently with your church community? They are energizing to be with, faith-filled, and supportive. But again we need to make the commitment, to participate actively with them and later on savor the pleasant results.

This list goes on and on and on. So negotiate some, soon to be, memorable time to observe and appreciate God's goodness in nature, your church community, your family, and your friends. Let your senses drink in the flavor and bounty given freely to us by God. Be careful. You may find new excitement in this venture and it will become exceedingly enticing and rewarding.

You will go out in joy and be led forth in peace; the mountains and hills will burst into song before you, and all the trees of the field will clap their hands. Isaiah 55:12

Hand in the Jar

We have all heard variations of the story of the little boy who went with his parents to the home of a very wealthy friend. The parents had reminded the boy to "look, but don't touch." The young lad wandered around the house while his parents were busy with the rich friend. As the parents were deep in conversation, they suddenly heard a blood-curdling scream coming from the next room. They rushed into the study and found the boy with his hand in a vase that was from the Ming Dynasty and worth fifty thousand dollars.

The parents and their friend tried numerous methods to extract the boy's hand from the vase without success. The friend, in exasperation, concluded there was nothing left to do but break the vase. Before the friend entered with the hammer, the parents again tried to find out how the boy got his hand stuck in the vase. The boy cried that he had looked into the vase, saw a nickel and grabbed it. When the parents convinced the boy to let go of the nickel, his hand easily came out of the vase. The boy had spent his time, efforts, and many tears trying to get something insignificant and not paying attention to the vase that was extremely valuable and irreplaceable. Perhaps we are not too dissimilar from the boy.

How often have we abandoned God's word and sacrament at church in order to be on time for a soccer practice, a luncheon date, or a baseball game? How frequently have we watched TV till late at night and then found ourselves too exhausted to pray? How quickly have we skipped reading God's word because we were too tired?

The justification for our misplaced priorities can and does go on and on. We all descend into the trap of spending our energies on things which are insignificant and ignoring the things that are extremely important. Whenever God has been put into second place in our priorities, we are guilty of worrying about meaningless trifles. When our daily events become all-consuming, we reach for the nickel rather than acknowledging the value of the vase. We need to stop and reevaluate our priorities. We should make certain God is the most important thing in our lives everything else being secondary. It requires time, effort, and dedication to get our priorities in proper order, but we must, or else we will be crying about the insignificant nickel like the little boy and ignoring God, who is extraordinarily more valuable and irreplaceable than any Ming vase.

Sow for yourselves righteousness, reap the fruit of unfailing love, and break up your unplowed ground; for it is time to seek the Lord, until he comes and showers righteousness on you. Hosea 10:12

This is what the Lord says to the house of Israel: "Seek me and live. Amos 5:4

Happy Meal

Deacon Al asked the kids at St. Elizabeth Ann Seton parish if they knew what he was holding up. They all recognized the package as a McDonald's Happy Meal. They knew it contained a hamburger, fries, and a prize. He then compared receiving the Eucharist, the body and blood of Jesus Christ, to a meal that provides nourishment and energy to our bodies. He also reminded the children to be careful of what they consumed because "you are what you eat." If you consume unhealthy things, it will reflect in your body's ability to grow and function.

How can this concept be helpful to adults? Do we heartily consume the Eucharist every Sunday and during other times during the year? Do we take advantage of Jesus' body to enliven our soul life? Do we drink the blood to quench our thirst for doing what is Christ-like? Do we use the Eucharist to continue our spiritual growth?

In order to be healthy Christians, we must be nourished. What better way to be nourished than with the Lord himself? The more we eat and digest, the better we are able to function as active and lively Christians. Besides Eurcharist the Lord provides other methods to be fed.

We can get our minimum daily requirements of soul calories by reading God's word. The scripture helps fortify our soul so we can successfully repel the attacks of Satan. It supplies the energy we need to grow up strong in our faith and strengthens our resolve against temptations. It is a vitamin that makes sure all our spiritual nutritional needs are met.

Other spiritual energy sources are the sacraments, our fellow walkers in the faith, religious music, uplifting retreats, and movies on the lives saintly people. God provides a bounty of means to strengthen, encourage, and stimulate the growth of our soul life. But we need to take advantage of them. Vitamins, just like God's word, are of no value unless they are consumed and internalized. On the shelf they are powerless to increase and strengthen our soul muscles.

Too often we get our food from trans-fat sources which are not advantageous for the body. Just like high-calorie foods that are not beneficial to the body, many daily activities are not beneficial to the soul. Look at your activities to discover if your activities and life style are nutritional.

Do our friends provide the vitamins we need as Christians? Do the movies and TV programs we watch provide healthy supplements to our souls, or are they like trans-fats, sweet to the taste but empty of nutritional value?

Are the books and music choices we make encouraging growth and life, or do they push us toward lethargy and decay? Do we get our sustenance from positive activities, or do we get our fill of empty calories from activities that neither promote growth nor encourage us to become better Christians? Remember we are what we eat. We can either fill ourselves with what is healthy for us or consume things that are not. The growth and health of our souls is dependent on our choices.

If we find our souls filled with trans-fat and unhealthy food then it is essential to begin change. Start the easy way. Go to church. Read the scriptures beforehand, and digest their message. Become actively involved in the Liturgy. Stay for the entire time being sure to consume every morsel of nourishment.

Next find some time for Sacred Scripture. Open up and close your day in meditation with books such as *Living Faith or Meditations.* It only takes a few minutes of your day. After a while you will find that the time you spend in prayer and contemplation will continue to expand because of your of your desire for adequate nourishment.

Continue to enlarge your circle of people who are encouragers of soul growth. Check out some movies and music they have found nourishing. Listen to their music and see if you would want to purchase some for yourself.

Start on a well-thought-out program to strengthen your spiritual muscles. Your church has many resources that might just be the vitamins you need to promote healthy growth and avoid the trans-fat material found everywhere in the secular world. The earlier you internalize your new habits the sooner you will change into the lean and agile Christian you were meant to become when you were created by God.

The Lord has provided all the means necessary for strong and healthy souls but you must make the effort to use those avenues to your advantage. It all starts with the Eucharist and continues with his word, sacraments, church and faithful fellow Christians. If you are what you eat, then make sure you only put in your soul foods that are nourishing and life-giving, not filled with trans-fat like the Happy Meal.

If you remain in me and my words remain in you, ask for whatever you want and it will be done for you. By this is my father glorified, that you bear much fruit and become my disciples. As the father loves me, so I also love you. Remain in my love. John 15:7–9

Moreover, God is able to make every grace abundant for you, so that in all things, always having all you need, you may have an abundance for every good work. As it is written: "He scatters abroad, he gives to the poor; his righteousness endures forever." 2 Corinthians 9:8, 9

Jesus then said to those Jews who believed in him, "If you remain in my word, you will truly be my disciples, and you will know the truth, and the truth will set you free." They answered him, "We are descendants of Abraham and have never been enslaved to anyone. How can you say, 'You will become free'?" Jesus answered them, "Amen, amen, I say to you, everyone who commits sin is a slave of sin. A slave does not remain in a household forever, but a son always remains. So if a son frees you, then you will truly be free. John 8:31–36

Holy Hands

In the song "Holy Hands," one line states, "he works through these hands, so these hands are holy." Wow! Our hands are holy because we do the work of the Lord. We are his presence to others on earth.

So when you have given a person a hug when they really need one, you are doing God's work. Building a porch or cabinet for a neighbor because you have the skills is a sacred act. Using your hands to help someone move their furniture to a new house or apartment is another holy act, an act that requires your blessed hands.

Too often we think our actions have to be remarkable to be holy. If they are done for the honor and glory of God, or they are Christ-like actions to help others, those acts are truly precious. If we allow God to work through our hands, they are blessed.

That means many, many things we do with our hands, or feet, or heart can be sacred actions. If they imitate Christ's message to love, they are holy. The opportunities we have to perform blessed acts are as numerous as the grains of sand on the sea or the stars in the skies—so numerous only God can keep track of them. Don't worry about how big the actions are, but rather concentrate on how often we use our holy hands in the service of others.

God is not unjust; he will not forget your work and the love you have shown him as you have helped his people and continue to help them. Hebrews 6:10

Suppose a brother or sister is without clothes and daily food. If one of you says to him, "Go, I wish you well; keep warm and well fed," but does nothing about his physical needs, what good is it? In the same way, faith by itself, if it is not accompanied by action, is dead. James 2:15–17

Humility and Defects of Character

Humility: the quality or state of being humble in spirit; freedom from pride or arrogance in the face of what we do not understand.

Are you aware of your defects of character? We all have them. We are human and are less than perfect which means we have areas of our lives than need to be worked on from time to time.

Our faults remind us that we require God's grace. Without his grace the defects will not disappear because we do not have the ability to remove them on our own.

How do we convert these defects to positive patterns? First of all we must accept them as they are part of our makeup. Once we have accepted and identified them, it is time to offer them up to God. We plead with him to provide the graces to reverse our behavior, patterns, and attitude. Since these changes are ongoing request for God's help and guidance will require constant prayer. Our heartfelt prayer will eventually lead to modification and correction.

God will shower us with the graces we need in his time and using his magnificently efficient method. We cannot impose our will or timetable for adaptation and improvement on God. He does the changing, while we are the channel to which the improvement will occur. Patience and persistence is required in our request for God's aid. Our humility in this process is shown by our realization that renewal and reshaping of defects originates from God. We cannot take credit for it any more than we can take credit for perfect weather conditions.

God also gives us opportunities to practice humility in the gifts and talents that he has freely endowed upon us. The abilities we are efficient and proficient in are precious jewels from God. If we enhance and develop our capabilities it is because God provides the nourishment and support to do that. All good and wonderful gifts come from God.

Professional athletes often point to the sky in acknowledgment of God's help in their performance. It is right and just that they praise God for his blessings that allows them to succeed on the playing field. We should also point to God and thank him for his generosity in our lives

God does requires us to apply our talents in a fit manner. They are to be applied to provide assistance and encouragement to those less capable than ourselves. We cannot waste our talents by being lazy or inconsiderate. If we do not put to use our abilities, we are rejecting God's wonderful present to us. He would not have given us these particular gifts if he didn't intend for us to apply them. The more talents we are given, the greater amount of benefits we can provide for others. If we don't sharpen and apply out skills, some need will go unfulfilled. If we don't develop them and share them, some person or institution will be lacking in the means to adequately support the needy.

 As humans we need to acknowledge both our strengths and failings. We should appreciate God's powerful role in our lives giving thanks and praise to him for our fortunate situations. Our humility is also displayed when we accept God as our omnipresent source of adaptation and modification He is always the most desirable and permanent solution available in our quest to obliterate our defects of character and develop fully into loving and caring people.

Do not let this book of the law (Bible) depart from your lips. Recite it by day and by night, that you may carefully observe all that is written in it; then you will attain your goal; then you will succeed. I command you: be strong and steadfast! Do not fear nor be dismayed, for the Lord, your God, is with you wherever you go. Joshua 1:8–11

I will instruct you and show you the way you should walk, give you counsel with my eye upon you. Psalm 32:8

All scripture is inspired by God and is useful for teaching, for refutation, for correction, and for training in righteousness, so that one who belongs to God may be competent, equipped for every good work. 2 Timothy 3:16, 17

The valiant one whose steps are guided by the Lord who will delight in his way, may stumble, but he will never fall, for the Lord holds his hand. Psalm 37:23, 24

If Politicians

If our politicians received our prayerful support as much as our money who knows what the positive changes there might be on their attitude and legislation.

Ask and it will be given to you; seek and you will find; knock and the door will be opened to you. For everyone who asks receives; he who seeks finds; and to him who knocks, the door will be opened. Which of you, if his son asks for bread, will give him a stone? Or if he asks for a fish, will give him a snake? If you, then, though you are evil, know how to give good gifts to your children, how much more will your father in heaven give good gifts to those who ask him! Matthew 7:7–11

You will pray to him, and he will hear you, and you will fulfill your vows. What you decide on will be done, and light will shine on your ways. Job 22:27, 28

If you believe, you will receive whatever you ask for in prayer." Matthew 21:22

Therefore confess your sins to each other and pray for each other so that you may be healed. The prayer of a righteous man is powerful and effective. James 5:16

Call to me and I will answer you and tell you great and unsearchable things you do not know. Jeremiah 33:3

Make some room in your prayer life to include the people who represent us in government. Pray that they act with integrity and with the concerns of the people in mind rather than their own political welfare. Pray constantly because God's support is required every day.

I Want to Talk to You
—God

Perhaps you have seen one of the creative highway signs by Christianity Oasis reminding us that God is important in our lives and we should be aware of his presence. These signs should nudge us into thinking on what we are doing, and should do, when it comes to knowing God.

One way to get to know God is to be aware of his presence—in others words, prayer. We need to pray and pray. The more we do that the more we will understand God. Like anything in life we need to practice to become good at it. So pray often.

Then you will call upon me and come and pray to me, and I will listen to you. Jeremiah 29:12

One excellent way to pray is to read the Bible. Become familiar with it. Read commentaries on what you have read. Spend time thinking about how the readings apply to your life.

Do not let this Book of the Law depart from your mouth; meditate on it day and night, so that you may be careful to do everything written in it. Then you will be prosperous and successful. Joshua 1:8

We also need to share with others. What talents do you have that you have been willing to share in your church? Have you let your light shine among your friends? Practice sharing yourself with your family, friends, and church.

Consequently, you are no longer foreigners and aliens, but fellow citizens with God's people and members of God's household, built on the foundation of the apostles and prophets, with Christ Jesus himself as the chief cornerstone. In him the whole building is joined together and rises to become a holy temple in the Lord. And in him you too are being built together to become a dwelling in which God lives by his Spirit. Ephesians 2:19–22

Always be open to the presence of God because like the billboard reminds us that God wants to talk to us.

Jesus Loves the Little Children

Jesus loves the little children
All the children of the world
Jesus loves the little children
Red or yellow, black or white
They are precious in His sight
Jesus loves the little children of the world.

This introduction to Ray Stevens's song "Everything is Beautiful" should remind us that God loves us dearly, like little children, like special and precious gifts. God created us in his image and could not love us any more than he does.

Do little children get into mischief? Do they disobey their parents? Do they disregard the rules of society? Do they make poor choices? The answer is yes to all of the above. But our father loves us so completely he forgives us our sins and provides every opportunity to keep us in his loving arms. Could we ask for anything more?

We are those children. We make all those mistakes. We adopt poor choices and unhealthy decisions. But God will always welcome us back, forgive us, and forget our sins. A mother may "forget" her children, but God has promised never to forget us or leave us orphaned. We are carved on the palm of God's hand. Forever and a day he will love and cherish and forgive us.

Like young children we also need to rejoice and be joyful, forget the cares of the world and enjoy being who we are, children of God. So pay attention to little children and learn from them. Rediscover how to be carefree. Behold the wonders of the world God has created. Trust in your loving father and creator. Open your eyes to the unconditional love of your God.

The promise is for you and your children and for all who are far off—for all whom the Lord our God will call. Acts 2:39

Leaf Blower

Life is like a leaf blower. It blows us around in what seems like a disorganized and chaotic manner—here and there and everywhere. But God is the leaf blower. It may look like there is no meaning to the scattering of the leaves but a method is in place.

God has us mingle with others. These chance meetings of one with another can affect our lives. We meet others, interact with them and then continue on our journey. Some leaves are with us a long time and some for only a brief period. Some become stuck together and ride the streams of air from the leaf blower. Whatever our encounters, long or short, they provide us with companionship, different concepts and ideas, and a variety in size, shape, and color. The mighty leaf blower directs the current in certain patterns for a desired goal.

And what is the goal? It is our salvation. God wants us together with him in the everlasting kingdom he has prepared for us.

What happens to the piles of leaves? They are burned or put into a compost pile to wither and decay. We shall die just like the leaves.

Just as trees start new growth in the spring God will have us reborn at the end of the earth, this new birth being everlasting, complete, and glorious. No longer will we be part of the circle of life and death. When we are recreated, there will only be life, love, and abundance.

If life seems disorganized and chaotic, remember the magnificent leaf blower. God will move us in the direction he desires. And in the end, we will be in the pile that will be resurrected and reborn to live eternally with our God in heaven.

For I am convinced that neither death nor life, neither angels nor demons, neither the present nor the future, nor any powers, neither height nor depth, nor anything else in all creation, will be able to separate us from the love of God that is in Christ Jesus our Lord. Romans 8:38, 39

The Lesson of the Starfish

A man was walking slowly along the beach. He noticed there were many starfish scattered along the shore. A violent storm had tossed them on the sand, and they were stranded and would probably die. The man thought he would throw them back into the ocean so they would have an opportunity to live. But then he thought, "There are just too many!" So he shrugged his shoulders and did nothing but continue silently on his journey along the beach.

As he continued strolling he came around a bend, he noticed a young child in the distance throwing starfish into the crashing waves. As the man approached the child, he said, "What difference will you make to the starfish? There are just too many to save. You can't rescue them all."

The young child quickly held up one starfish and with a smile proudly stated, "I will make a huge difference to this starfish. Because of me, it will have a chance at survival."

This story illustrates the fact that we are not called to rearrange the entire world, bring about global peace, and end famine in our lifetime. We are here to make a difference in the lives of the people we encounter, no matter how many or how few that happens to be.

God does the changing of people and events, and we only have to be ourselves and allow him to work through us. We can all confidently handle that task. Ask God for his help, guidance, and patience in your efforts to be a force of change in your unique corner of the world.

I tell you the truth, anyone who has faith in me will do what I have been doing. He will do even greater things than these, because I am going to the Father. John 14:12

Let it Shine

This little light of mine
I'm gonna let it shine.
This little light of mine
I'm gonna let it shine.
Let it shine, let it shine,
Let it shine.

All around the world
I'm gonna let it shine.
All around the world
I'm gonna let it shine.
Let it shine, let it shine,
Let it shine.

These words by Harry Dixon Loes remind me of a little story told by Herman Gockel in *Give Your Life a Lift. H*e tells of a little girl traveling with her mother and looking at beautiful cathedrals. In one cathedral the little girl was enthralled by the stained glass windows of the saints. When she arrived home, the little girl told her mother who the saints were. The mother listened as the girl told her that saints were people who let the light shine through just like the stained glass windows of the cathedral did. Wow! Is that true?

We, as saints in training, are called to spread the Good News of God's love for his people. That ability has to come from within. With God firmly implanted in our souls and hearts, we can let his light shine through us. Because of our actions, we show the world God's love, concern, faithfulness, and grace. Our daily living speaks volumes to others as to our faith and beliefs.

God will nourish us to be effective "doers of the word" and will be our fuel to provide the will and the energy to preach the word both orally and with actions. We need to make sure that the energy source is active by reading God's word, receiving his sacraments, and communicating often with him in prayer.

With God's energy we can let his light shine through us. We can spread the Good News, and we can do it in our own unique style. We can be ourselves—no putting on airs or trying to be something we aren't. We just need to be natural, and God will do the rest. Are you ready to let the light shine through?

In the same way, let your light shine before men, that they may see your good deeds and praise your Father in heaven. Matthew 5:16

Light

It is amazing what a little light can do. If you are anything like me, once the lights are turned off at night, you have trouble telling distances, finding how far you have walked, and knowing where you are. You grope your way to the bed or the bathroom. Sometimes you bump into a wall because you are not sure of your location. You move gingerly because everything seems so distant. You become very timid in your actions when you cannot see clearly.

Life's challenges are like that. We move cautiously because we don't know where we are or how far and in what direction we are going. We are not "sure footed" because of the lack of light.

How do we turn on the light that will help us move confidently and with a sense of direction? It is simple. We need to seek the great light, God, for assistance and guidance. The more we know about God, the more we will see things clearly. As God graciously enters our lives, the better able we are to maneuver through the difficulties we encounter on our life's journey. The necessary and indispensable key is God.

Take time each day, each hour, each minute to include God in all your activities. Read about him in scripture. Listen to his advice during church services. Sing about God with Christian CDs or music videos. Pursue his majestic light so you can also be light to others.

The more we are actively involved in prayer the clearer the picture of life becomes. As God increasingly enters our life the greater light shines on our journey and confidence builds in us. We will no longer grope in the dark, trying to figure out where we are and where we are headed. God will always be our lighthouse and beacon of safety in the rough and challenging waters of life.

But you will receive power when the Holy Spirit comes on you; and you will be my witnesses in Jerusalem, and in all Judea and Samaria, and to the ends of the earth. Acts 1:8

You are the light of the world. A city on a hill cannot be hidden. Neither do people light a lamp and put it under a bowl. Instead they put it on its stand, and it gives light to everyone in the house. In the same way, let your light shine before men, that they may see your good deeds and praise your father in heaven. Matthew 5:14–16

The Lobster

There once was a lobster named Steve who was very content in his tank at Empire Fish Market. Life was good, and the lobster was happy. One bright spring day a lady named Jeanne came to pick out a lobster for a meal she was going to prepare for her boyfriend.

Jeanne took the lobster home and placed him in a pot of warm water. Steve immediately disliked the new surroundings. The water was much warmer than he was accustomed. It was uncomfortable, to say the least. But Steve decided to make the most of the situation. After a few minutes he adjusted to the new temperature.

Jeanne came back half an hour later and turned up the dial on the stove. Again Steve became hot, uncomfortable, and somewhat irritable. He did not appreciate this new twist in his environment at all. But he was determined to handle the situation. Eventually Steve became accustomed to the higher water temperature and began to relax.

After coming back from some chores Jeanne decided the lobster's water was not warm enough, so she turned up the heat another notch. Larry didn't seem to notice the change as much as in the past. His skin felt a little prickly, but he just put the thought of the pain out of his mind and tried to rest.

Since the meal was not far off, Jeanne went to the stove and increased the heat a few more degrees. It was now extremely hot. Poor Steve just closed his eyes and didn't pay attention to the latest adjustment in the temperature. The bubbles in the water seem to be dancing around the very pink lobster. He was almost cooked and ready for the evening meal.

What can we derive from the lobster story? If we place ourselves in situations where we are uncomfortable, hot, and irritable, we should adopt steps to alter the environment. If we don't, we eventually will be like Larry, cooked, and we won't know how it happened.

It might be the people you associate with on a daily basis. Are they positive, motivating, and life-giving? Or are they the kind who belittle people, making themselves feel superior only by making others feel inferior? It might be people who use foul language or do risqué things. We know they aren't right, but we don't relate to them our feelings, worrying more about being accepted rather than being upright.

Do we associate with people who grumble? Is their attitude negative? Police officers who deal with people in prison who lie, cheat, use obscenities, and treat others with distain on a daily basis can often incorporate the same traits of the inmates if they aren't careful. They begin treating inmates as non-people and act increasingly like the prisoners.

We should diligently look at our environment, our friends and associates, and the institutions we belong to, and judge if they are positive and Christ-like or negative and life destroying. If we are not careful, the lobster will not be the only thing that gets cooked.

All the prophets testify about him that everyone who believes in him receives forgiveness of sins through his name." Acts 10:43

And that is what some of you were. But you were washed, you were sanctified, you were justified in the name of the Lord Jesus Christ and by the Spirit of our God "Everything is permissible for me"—but not everything is beneficial. "Everything is permissible for me"—but I will not be mastered by anything. "Food for the stomach and the stomach for food"—but God will destroy them both. The body is not meant for sexual immorality, but for the Lord, and the Lord for the body. By his power God raised the Lord from the dead, and he will raise us also. Do you not know that your bodies are members of Christ himself? Shall I then take the members of Christ and unite them with a prostitute? Never! 1 Corinthians 6:11–15

Therefore tell the people: This is what the Lord Almighty says: "Return to me," declares the Lord Almighty, "and I will return to you," says the Lord Almighty. Zechariah 1:3

The mind of sinful man is death, but the mind controlled by the Spirit is life and peace; the sinful mind is hostile to God. It does not submit to God's law, nor can it do so. Those controlled by the sinful nature cannot please God. You, however, are controlled not by the sinful nature but by the Spirit, if the Spirit of God lives in you. And if anyone does not have the Spirit of Christ, he does not belong to Christ. But if Christ is in you, your body is dead because of sin, yet your spirit is alive because of righteousness. Romans 8:6–10

Thanks to Dr. Manley of Whitewater, who first told me about the story of the lobster.

Love, Humor, Wisdom, and God

God loves us dearly. We know that from the many graces he has sent to us. He also gave us Jesus to act as our scapegoat. Jesus suffered, died, and rose from the dead so we could be free of sin and heirs to God's kingdom. No greater love is there than one willing to give up his life for another. No greater love could God show than giving us Jesus as atonement for our sins.

God's love has no bounds, and his mercy is greater than any of our sins. He even loves us during the times when we think we are superior to others. I was reminded of this one day after receiving an e-mail from a friend. The e-mail listed quotes from famous people that were pretty stupid. One stated the person loved California because he practically grew up in Phoenix. He must be pretty dimwitted to think Phoenix is in California. The crux of the e-mail was that if these famous people could say such ignorant things, then we must be pretty intelligent. We might feel superior to them and even ignore our own faults and failings.

When I began to feel superior to those famous people, I think God gently reminded me of some of the foolish things I have done. One was when I tried to dye my hair blond by using bleach. Not only did I not change my hair color, I ended up with white spots on my plaid shorts. Not an intelligent thing to do. Later I used Sun-In hair coloring. It didn't work the first time, so I tried it again. Finally my hair color did change.

The only problem was that my hair was orange and not blond. Feeling embarrassed, I missed my brother and sister-in-law's tenth wedding anniversary. I then had to have my hair professionally dyed so I could attend my parents' fiftieth wedding anniversary the following week. I looked fine, but the hair was a darker color than usual, not having the shades and highlights of my natural shade of brown.

I also remembered the time my foot became stuck in a student chair while I was lecturing to my class. There was also the time I tried to re-light the furnace in the apartment building after it had gone out. Not knowing what I was doing, I ended up with singed eyebrows and face feeling grateful that it was not a serious injury, as it might have been. Reflecting on these incidents, I realized I am not superior to others and shouldn't try to make myself feel better by putting people down for their foibles. I have plenty of my own.

I appreciate that God must has a sense of humor. I bet he found amusing my bright orange hair. But his love was there for me nonetheless. And now that plenty of time has passed, I can see the humor in it too. The more humor we can see in situations, the better we can put them into proper perspective and the less likely we will be judgmental when it comes to dealing with others and their abilities or lack of abilities.

God does want us to learn from our experiences, to grow and change, and to accrue wisdom. When we read about God in the Bible, receive the sacraments, and pray, he guarantees we can obtain wisdom.

If any of you lacks wisdom, he should ask God, who gives generously to all without finding fault, and it will be given to him. James 1:5

Wisdom is supreme; therefore get wisdom. Though it cost all you have, get understanding. Proverbs 4:7

Growing from our experiences, even orange hair, and allowing God to aid us in our development will give us wisdom. That wisdom should help us deal with others in a Christ-like manner. We will be able to laugh at our mistakes, learn from them, and cherish others, with all their own particular faults and failings.

Everything in our life begins and ends with God. He gives us life, guides us on our journey, laughs at our stupidity, loves us all the time, and provides us with the means to obtain wisdom and even more importantly eternal life. What else could we ask for from God? So remember God loves you. Enjoy your miscues, learn from them, find humor in them, and then seek God's wisdom to evolve and mature into an ever increasingly loving individual.

Behold, I stand at the door and knock. If anyone hears my voice and opens the door, (then) I will enter his house and dine with him, and he with me. I will give the victor the right to sit with me on my throne, as I myself first won the victory and sit with my Father on his throne. Revelation 3:20, 21

I am the friend of all who fear you, of all who keep your precepts. The earth, Lord, is filled with your love; teach me your laws. Psalm 119:63, 64

God is faithful, and by him you were called to fellowship with his Son, Jesus Christ our Lord. 1 Corinthians 1:9

Meat and Potatoes

When I was growing up, we often had a meal where the potatoes and the meat were the main parts of the meal—the essentials around which the rest of the meal was organized. I wonder if we shouldn't think of God in the same way. Is He the meat and potatoes of our life? Is God the center of our life on which we base our thoughts and actions?

Is my job more important than God? Or do I include him in all the decisions I make there? Do I think of what Jesus would do in any situation I encounter? How are my decisions made? Is prayer part of my workplace? Do I thank God for the fact that I have a job? How might I bring my Christian ethics into my dealings with fellow employees?

My relationships with family and friends are important and supporting to me. Is God one of those relationships? What order or rank is he in importance compared to the rest of the people? I know God is with me always, but can others tell by what I say and do that he is helping me, encouraging me and sustaining me?

Do I take God on vacation with me or do I leave him at church where I visit him once in a while? How can I make sure that I thank God for his goodness and appreciate the beauty of his creations? Where will I set aside an ample amount of time to communicate with him in prayer?

God wants to be the center, or substance, of our lives, just like meat and potatoes are the main part of a meal. God is not a dessert to be relished at the end of the meal. He should not be an insignificant part of the proceedings. He should be the epicenter of our lives, the substance on which everything else depends. If I take away the milk or coffee, the dessert, and the vegetables but have the meat and potatoes, I still have a substantial meal. If you take away my job, my friends, or my position in the community, I still am in great shape if I have God as my Lord and Savior. The choice is mine. Is God the meat and potatoes in my life or not?

Then Jesus declared, "I am the bread of life. He who comes to me will never go hungry, and he who believes in me will never be thirsty. John 6:35

For God so loved the world that he gave his one and only Son, that whoever believes in him shall not perish but have eternal life. John 3:16

I have come into the world as a light, so that no one who believes in me should stay in darkness. John 12:46

Mini Bible

Did you ever wish you could carry the Bible around with you all the time? It would be a handy reference any time we would need it. We could take a break and quickly read a passage. That short reading might be just what we need at the moment. Then we could get back to your daily routine.

Well, it is not just the Bible thumpers who can have the Bible close at hand. With modern science we have been able to reduce the Bible to a handy, dandy, one page compendium of all that is necessary for us in life. Sounds fantastic, doesn't it? For just thirty-nine dollars, this fantastic source of knowledge can be yours. Actually, you don't need to even spend a dime. It can be yours absolutely free. No catch. No hidden print. No slight of hand. A one-page Bible can be yours right now.

All you need to do is summarize all that is in the Bible into one simple concept. Our Lord, Jesus, has already done that for us. He has told us, through Mark, what the two commandments we need to follow are.

"The most important one," answered Jesus, "is this: 'Hear, O Israel, the Lord our God, The Lord is one. Love the Lord your God with all your heart and with all your soul and with all your mind and with all your strength.' The second is this: 'Love your neighbor as yourself.' There is no commandment greater than these." Mark 12:29–31

It is so simple, but not easy. All we need to do is love God above all else, and our neighbors as ourselves. Where do we start? How do we continue? Will God give us the strength to fulfill that commandment? The answer is yes. Humbly pray to God to provide the insight and the commitment to love both God and our fellow human beings. Pray for patience. Pray for strength. Pray for endurance. Pray always.

Now you can relax. You don't need to carry the Bible to work (although it wouldn't hurt). You don't need to memorize long passages. You do need to follow the two commandments the best way you can. You do need to pray. You do need to realize God is with you always. You can do it all with you mini Bible.

For more in-depth reading and sustenance, you should read God's word. Although the mini Bible is handy, it is not a substitute for continued inspiration by daily reading of the Bible.

All scripture is inspired by God and is useful for teaching, for refutation, for correction, and for training in righteousness, so that one who belongs to God may be competent equipped for every good work. 2 Timothy 16, 17

Every word of God is pure; he is a shield to those who take refuge in him. Proverbs 30:5

"All flesh is like grass, and all its glory like the flower of the field; the grass withers, and the flower wilts; but the word of the Lord remains forever." 1 Peter 1:24, 25

Amen, I say to you, this generation will not pass away until all these things have taken place. Heaven and earth will pass away, but my words will not pass away. Mark 13:30, 31

A Month of Sundays

If we had a month of Sundays, how the world would improve? We would spend more quality time with our families. The more quality time we spend with the family, the greater chances are there would be less crime, fewer low self-esteem problems, fewer drug problems, and less promiscuous sex in our young people. TV would have better programs because people would demand that TV be appropriate for all viewers, not just adults or extremely liberal people.

Our social life would improve. We would be rejuvenated because we would be relaxed. Thus the projects we worked on would benefit because of our new energy and enthusiasm. They would be completed on a timely basis.

But most important of all our spiritual life would be enhanced. Instead of concentrating on God for one hour out of the week, we would be spending at least sixty minutes every day communicating with God. Oh, how our worship would improve! How our communications skills with God would develop! God would be an active partner in our lives every day instead of just one day a week. What a difference that would make in our demeanor and the way we would handle our problems. Just think of the possibilities a month of Sundays could produce!

Alas, we don't have a month of Sundays. But we can actively begin the effort to include God in our every-day lives and invite him to participate with us in all of our decisions. We should pray for his support and guidance continually so God would be our partner and confidant instead of a person who is more like an invited guest—someone we treat well but is not part of our innermost being. The more involved God is in our daily actions the easier it becomes to continue and expand that involvement. That could motivate dramatic and healthy alterations in our lives!

We can begin today to find ways to include God fully into our actions. We can start the expansion of our dealings with God so that one day we would be acting like there really is a month of Sundays.

Whatever you do, work at it with all your heart, as working for the Lord, not for men, since you know that you will receive an inheritance from the Lord as a reward. It is the Lord Christ you are serving. Colossians 3:23, 24

Be imitators of God, therefore, as dearly loved children and live a life of love, just as Christ loved us and gave himself up for us as a fragrant offering and sacrifice to God. Ephesians 5:1, 2

Guard my life, for I am devoted to you. You are my God; save your servant who trusts in you. Have mercy on me, O Lord, for I call to you all day long. Bring joy to your servant, for to you, O Lord, I lift up my soul. You are forgiving and good, O Lord, abounding in love to all who call to you. Hear my prayer, O Lord; listen to my cry for mercy. In the day of my trouble I will call to you, for you will answer me. Among the gods there is none like you, O Lord; no deeds can compare with yours. Psalm 86:2–8

No Big Deal

When we look at ourselves and see that we need to make some changes in our lives, do we get nervous? Do we look at ourselves and think it would be too difficult to make major adjustments in our lives? We know that God wants us to improve and develop, but maybe that change is too much for us to handle. Maybe God expects too much from us.

This is to my father's glory, that you bear much fruit, showing yourselves to be my disciples. John 15:8

When we look at where we think we should be and where we are, we could get discouraged. It seems like the task is way beyond us. It can't possibly be done. We would be right. It can't be done if we look at the end result compared to where we are. The change would be too dramatic and would appear be something only a superior person could do. Because we are not super people, we may feel like we cannot make this change.

What we need to do is look at where we think we should be and see what steps are essential to accomplish that goal. The trick is to start small. Don't look at the end result, but look at the minute reform we can make between today and tomorrow. That incremental change could be like the difference between the words "better" and "bitter." The difference is only one letter (a small change), but the end result is quite spectacular.

If we look at ourselves and realize we need to lose forty pounds, it might seem like an insurmountable task. But losing two or three pounds is no big deal. We all think we can do that much. If we think small, we lose the two pounds and then try to stay at that point for a while. After a period of being down those two pounds, we can strive to lose another two pounds (no big deal). The same process begins: we reduce our body weight by two pounds, get used to that weight for a while, and then make an effort to lose two additional pounds. After a length of time we would find out we have lost the forty pounds. The difference is we worked to improve ourselves in tiny steps.

In our spiritual life, we need steps that are no big deal to us. If we change a little this year and a little next year, by the end of thirty years we would have made significant modifications in our life. It is all in the way we analyze our problems. Do we gaze at the entire problem, or do we break it down into manageable parts?

Wait for the Lord; be strong and take heart and wait for the Lord. Psalm 27:14

Think, for example, of reading the entire Bible. That sounds like a mighty task. But if we spent fifteen minutes a day reading the Bible (no big deal) we could read the entire Bible in a year or so. The trick, again, is to break the task into workable steps. After a period of time we will have completed something that looked to be too difficult to accomplish.

Obey me, and I will be your God and you will be my people. Walk in all the ways I command you, that it may go well with you. Jeremiah 7:23

Besides breaking our difficulties or changes into manageable bites, we must include God in the process. God's energy and grace is essential to help us change. God's words and encouragement are necessary in our day-to-day efforts when it is hard to see any improvement. God's courage

231

and insight helps us make those small, incremental steps that eventually lead to a major change in our lives.

Therefore, I urge you, brothers, in view of God's mercy, to offer your bodies as living sacrifices, holy and pleasing to God—this is your spiritual act of worship. Do not conform any longer to the pattern of this world, but be transformed by the renewing of your mind. Then you will be able to test and approve what God's will is—his good, pleasing and perfect will. Romans 12:1, 2

We can start today by projecting to where we would like to be in the future. What steps are necessary to promote modifications? How often will we find it necessary to pray for God's help, guidance, and strength? Who can support us in my efforts to change? How will we know we have completed the alterations necessary to be the persons God wants us to be? How can we celebrate the pint-sized changes we make in a day? A week? A month?

Do not be anxious about anything, but in everything, by prayer and petition, with thanksgiving, present your requests to God. Philippians 4:6

When we critically examine our lives and the challenges God gives us, we can become bitter, or we can choose to become better. We can break down our challenges into small changes, or we can give up when we look at the monumental modifications we need to make. We can get the support and sustenance from God and our friends, or we can try to change on our own, which usually leads to no change and no growth. Bitter or better, the choice is ours. It's no big deal.

Those who hope in the Lord will renew their strength. They will soar on wings like eagles; they will run and not grow weary, they will walk and not be faint. Isaiah 40:31

And let us consider how we may spur one another on toward love and good deeds. Let us not give up meeting together, as some are in the habit of doing, but let us encourage one another—and all the more as you see the Day approaching. Hebrews 10:24, 25

For this very reason, make every effort to add to your faith goodness; and to goodness, knowledge; and to knowledge, self-control; and to self-control, perseverance; and to perseverance, godliness; and to godliness, brotherly kindness; and to brotherly kindness, love. 2 Peter 1:5, 6

Offerings of Love

When you think of it, isn't it the look of understanding in a friend's eyes or a gentle touch of genuine affection that heals our wounded hearts and opens us to love? No matter how insignificant our actions may seem, when they flow from the Spirit of Christ within us, they can transform the world. Terri Mifek

These words remind us not to be concerned with size and importance. That is what the world considers important, not God. We can't match the generosity of people like Bill Gates in terms of money. But we certainly can match the sincerity of anyone and their willingness to help others, no matter how much money or power they have.

God looks at the heart and not the ability to pay. God expects us to use the gifts he has given us, not the ones that belong to others. We are to share our unique gifts and talents according to those amounts given to us. If we are poor it matters not. We can share a friendly smile, a special batch of cookies or favorite pie, a warm handshake, or a gentle hug. God provides us with so many opportunities to share. We just need to look at what we can offer and then be willing to give whatever it is wholeheartedly. We all have the ability to do that. It is a matter of making the choice to enhance our ability to share God's gifts with others or to jealously hoard them for ourselves.

As he looked up, Jesus saw the rich putting their gifts into the temple treasury. He also saw a poor widow put in two very small copper coins. "I tell you the truth," he said, "this poor widow has put in more than all the others. All these people gave their gifts out of their wealth; but she out of her poverty put in all she had to live on." Luke 21:1–4

Take time enjoying being the poor widow. We can't match corporate giants or rich movie or TV stars, but we can maximize our abilities in whatever from God has blessed us with. If we look inside ourselves we can discover what we can do and uncover ways to share those abilities and talents. We are limited, God is not. We should allow God to carefully and gently mold us into the cheerful people who provides offerings of love to others.

Open My Heart, Lord

Open my heart, Lord. Help me to love like you. Jesse Manibusan

My sister is calling to complain again. Do I really have time to listen to her? There is another beggar on the street. Do I really have to give him something? How many times to do I have say no to my child? Doesn't he get what no means? Another function at church this month? I already have done my share. I won't do this one. Open my heart, Lord. Help me to love like you.

I am so angry at my cousin. I swear I will never talk to her again. Lend my brother money again? I'll never get it back. When will he learn responsibility? Oops, the grocer gave me too much change. Lucky me. I give twice as much as my sister does to the church. Why can't she be as generous as me? Open my heart, Lord. Help me to love like you.

Do any of these comments make you uncomfortable? Good. God wants us to seriously consider what we are doing and how it affects others. Can we do a better job? Can we be more caring instead of worrying about our own selfish feelings? Do we need a change of attitude? Are we looking at situations with the tender disposition of Jesus? Whenever we react to people, comment on situations, and plan strategies in our life, we must consider how loving we are. Often a concerned and helpful reaction to the problem is not what comes to mind, but it should.

We need to look at our actions and pray for guidance. God's help is essential in any decision we make. If we opt for an unhealthy decision, we need to correct the misstep in the best possible way. We should constantly analyze why we are doing the actions and reactions we are doing. If it is because of a loving attitude, great. If not, we ought to petition God for his assistance in order to revamp our procedures and attitudes.

Start small by deciding to do one or two new acts of kindness for people we associate with often. Once the new pattern is ingrained, we can expand the practice into more and more decisions we make. We have a whole lifetime to get comfortable with and perfect the concept of opening our heart completely to the Lord.

If we live, we live to the Lord; and if we die, we die to the Lord. So, whether we live or die, we belong to the Lord. Romans 14:8

And so we know and rely on the love God has for us. God is love. Whoever lives in love lives in God, and God in him. We love because he first loved us. 1 John 4:16, 19

And now these three remain: faith, hope and love. But the greatest of these is love. 1 Corinthians 13:13

Opportunity

For you were once darkness, but now you are light in the Lord. Live as children of light (for the fruit of the light consists in all goodness, righteousness and truth) and find out what pleases the Lord. Have nothing to do with the fruitless deeds of darkness, but rather expose them. For it is shameful even to mention what the disobedient do in secret. But everything exposed by the light becomes visible, for it is light that makes everything visible.

This is why it is said: "Wake up, O sleeper, rise from the dead, and Christ will shine on you." Ephesians 5:8–14

Where and when have you been light to someone else? Can you plan ahead so you will be ready for your next opportunity to be beacon for someone? Seek God's abundant graces through prayer to take advantage of your next chance to share your light with someone else.

In all your ways acknowledge him, and he will make your paths straight. Proverbs 3:6

Yet I am always with you; you hold me by my right hand. You guide me with your counsel, and afterward you will take me into glory. Psalm 73:23, 24

The Oyster

There once was an oyster
Whose story I tell
Who found that some sand
Had got into his shell;
It was only a grain,
But it gave him great pain.
For oysters have feelings
Although they're so plain.

Now, did he berate
The harsh workings of fate
That had brought him
To such a deplorable state?
No —he said to himself
As he lay on a shell,
Since I cannot remove it,
I shall try to improve it.
Now the years have rolled around,
As the years always do,
And he came to his ultimate
Destiny-stew.

And the small grain of sand

That bothered him so
Was a beautiful pearl
All richly aglow.
Now the tale has a moral;
For isn't it grand
What an oyster can do
With a morsel of sand?

What couldn't we do
If we'd only begin
With some of the things (persons)
That get under our skin.

David Colen

Lord, help me, with your grace, to treat all human beings like a pearl rather than a grain of sand. It won't be easy, but with your help, I will improve. I will try to remember in all situations, "What Would Jesus do?"

Pain and Suffering in Life

One of the most fascinating aspects of human behavior is that we are not able to free ourselves from bad experiences until we learn from them. Tragedies cling to us until we determine their lessons. Then we free ourselves. Once we learn what is to be learned, we move on. Robert J. Furey

Pain and suffering are part of our life as human beings. Sometimes we blame God for the troubles in our life. Why is he doing that to us? We haven't done anything wrong. Why us? Too often we don't realize that something good will come out of the bad experience. It may take a long time before we figure out what that is, but it is there.

So we shouldn't be so quick to bemoan our fate. Situations may not be pleasant, our health may not be perfect, and we may not know how the event will turn out. What we need to do is trust in our God. Trust that he knows what is best for us, that he will see us through any situation we encounter and that the difficulty will ultimately be for our benefit.

"For my thoughts are not your thoughts, neither are your ways my ways," declares the Lord. "As the heavens are higher than the earth, so are my ways higher than your ways and my thoughts than your thoughts. Isaiah 55:8, 9

A righteous man may have many troubles, but the Lord delivers him from them all. Psalm 34:19

And we know that in all things God works for the good of those who love him, who have been called according to his purpose. Romans 8:28

Paying Attention

When someone is talking to us, we have the option of listening to the person or paying attention to them. If we are listening, we are hearing what the person has to say. But we may not be making a conscious effort to take in the message. We may let other sounds or sights distract us from the information we are receiving. Listening takes minimal effort.

If we are paying attention to the words, we are concentrating on the message letting it soak into our being. We attempt to keep our mind focused, our ears open, and our minds eager to take in any valuable information that comes to us. Paying attention could also involve planning to use the concepts being presented to enrich and change our life and actions. Paying attention requires our full involvement.

Jesus often said in the Bible that we need to pay attention rather than just listen to his words. He used the phrase "amen, amen I say to you." He invited his audience to focus in on what he said, remove any distractions that would prevent them from knowing the concepts being presented, and incorporate those ideas into their daily existence. Too often the Pharisees listened to his words, ignored them, and didn't apply them as a means to rearrange their lives to match what God the father wanted them to be like. They listened but didn't pay attention.

Amen, amen, I say to you, we speak of what we know and we testify to what we have seen, but you people do not accept our testimony. If I tell you about earthly things and you do not believe, how will you believe if I tell you about heavenly things? No one has gone up to heaven except the one who has come down from heaven, the Son of Man. And just as Moses lifted up the serpent in the desert, so must the Son of Man be lifted up, so that everyone who believes in him may have eternal life. John 3:11–15

Do we listen at church or do we pay attention to what is being presented? Do we fully integrate ourselves into the service, removing distractions, putting ourselves into the moment, and asking ourselves how we will use the information presented to motivate us to grow and change? Paying attention takes enormous effort. How willing are we into putting forth that effort?

If we depart from church and enter the parking lot and become impatient with our fellow drivers, have we really paid attention to the message of the service? If we allow trivial issues in our daily lives to upset our decisions and actions, have we been intently paying attention to God's messages given to us that day?

For God is not unjust so as to overlook your work and the love you have demonstrated for his name by having served and continuing to serve the holy ones. We earnestly desire each of you to demonstrate the same eagerness for the fulfillment of hope until the end, so that you may not become sluggish, but imitators of those who, through faith and patience, are inheriting the promises. Hebrews 6:10–13

No, we are not perfect. Yes, sometimes we go through the motions and just listen to things being said to us. God does not ask us to be perfect on earth, but he does expect us to pay attention to him and put forth those concepts to change our perceptions and actions in each and every facet of our lives. God expects us to be "doers" of the Word and not just "hearers" of the Word.

Take time after a church service and see how and where those concepts presented can transform your life. Be an active participant during and after the presentation. Be in the moment, getting rid of distractions and concentrating on what is said and implied by the words. Try everything you can to pay attention for those words spoken apply to the people in the New Testament times but also us in our lives today.

Amen, I say to you, this generation will not pass away until all these things have taken place. Heaven and earth will pass away, but my words will not pass away. Matthew 24:34, 35

Afterward the other virgins (ten foolish virgins) came and said, "Lord, open the door for us!" But he said in reply, "Amen, I say to you, I do not know you." Therefore, stay awake, for you know neither the day nor the hour. Matthew 25:11–13

A Penny's Worth

Did you ever notice how people ignore pennies on the ground? Maybe they are passed by because they are worth very little. Maybe they aren't picked up because there are so many, and why bother with something so insignificant? Maybe the reward is not worth the exertion of bending down to pick them up. Maybe it is just laziness. Or it might even be that we don't notice them because we have other things on our mind.

Isn't it exciting to realize that God isn't like that? He loves us even though there are billions of us. We all look pretty much alike and react the same to similar situations. But to God, we are individuals with unique personalities, traits, talents, and gifts. He should know because God created us and adorned us with those gifts that make us who we are and who we are not.

To God we are anything but insignificant. He sent his only son to suffer and die for us. He would not have done that for something insignificant. Our value must be enormous for all the trials Jesus went through to save us from sin.

God does not overlook us or forget we are here. When it comes to our care, he is not lazy. God spends his days and nights watching over us, protecting us from harm, and showering us with love. He does spend the time to bend down and enter our lives, to encourage us, to renew us, to inspire us, and to console us.

Look at the penny. See how insignificant it is in our lives. Then take time to realize how valuable we are in God's eyes. A penny's worth is not valuable in our global economy, but to God we are not small and meaningless, but cherished and loved, something worth dying for.

Are not two sparrows sold for a penny? Yet not one of them will fall to the ground apart from the will of your father. And even the very hairs of your head are all numbered. So don't be afraid; you are worth more than many sparrows. Matthew 10:29–31

People Come and Go in Life, But God is Always With You—The One Constant Companion

God is our refuge and strength, an ever-present help in trouble. Therefore we will not fear, though the earth give way and the mountains fall into the heart of the sea, though its waters roar and foam and the mountains quake with their surging. Psalm 46:1–3

Though the mountains be shaken and the hills be removed, yet my unfailing love for you will not be shaken nor my covenant of peace be removed," says the Lord, who has compassion on you. Isaiah 54:10

Here I am! I stand at the door and knock. If anyone hears my voice and opens the door, I will come in and eat with him, and he with me. Revelation 3:20

Can a mother forget the baby at her breast and have no compassion on the child she has borne? Though she may forget, I will not forget you! See, I have engraved you on the palms of my hands; your walls are ever before me. Isaiah 49:15, 16

A lighthouse is a constant reminder of where land is and where safety lies. God is our lighthouse, reminding us where he is and how he will always be there to bring us safely home.

Pity Pot

This is my pity pot song. I don't plan to sing it very long. Yea. Mari Hang

It takes Mari Hang, the writer of the above song, less than a minute to sing the entire song. Maybe that is just about the right amount of time we should spend on feeling sorry for our selves.

Problems and difficulties will come into our lives many times before we enter the kingdom of heaven. It is very easy to feel sorry for our misfortune. Of course, the same kinds of things happen to others, but they are less severe or less traumatic than the things that happen to us. It should take us more time to get over them. Really? Having empathy for others and their difficult situations will put our trials in proper perspective – different than theirs but just as authentic.

When problems occur we are to turn to God for help and guidance.

Cast all your anxiety on him because he cares for you. 1 Peter 5:7

I lift up my eyes to the hills—where does my help come from? My help comes from the Lord, the Maker of heaven and earth. Psalm 121:1, 2

With God at our side, we can overcome any problem. If that is true, we should not spend much time in self-pity.

God asks us to do what we can and let him do the rest. We trust God will guide and support us until the problem is resolved in some way. We waste time and effort if we continue to worry about the problem. Letting God be in charge will reduce self-pity and bring peace to us.

I can do everything through him who gives me strength. Philippians 4:13

Those who hope in the Lord will renew their strength. They will soar on wings like eagles; they will run and not grow weary, they will walk and not be faint. Isaiah 40:31

So we should relax and bask in the knowledge that after we have done our part God will complete the task because nothing is impossible for him. God will complete the task in his manner and his timetable and will provide whatever response is needed and that should fill us with reassurance and peace.

Peace I leave with you; my peace I give you. I do not give to you as the world gives. Do not let your hearts be troubled and do not be afraid. John 14:27

We know that troubles will enter our lives, but with complete confidence in God our "pity pot" songs will be brief. Peace will fill our hearts and minds rather than worry and doubt. It is up to us. Trust in God and relax or depend on ourselves and become despondent and full of self-pity. The length of our song will be in direct proportion to our trust in God.

Pleasure and Guilt: Weapons of Satan, the Unholy Spirit

Satan has many weapons in his war against us and in his efforts to separate us from God. The devil encourages us to find pleasure in things we shouldn't. Mass media of today helps the devil to preach his message of "if it feels good, do it." "If everyone is doing it," another often used slogan of the devil, then the activity should be embraced wholeheartedly. Too often we fall into that devious trap and seek pleasure where we shouldn't and commit acts we know are not following God's teachings. We sin.

But the devil doesn't stop with just the sin, he refines his efforts to separate us from God by following up our offences with feelings of guilt. We have sinned, and feel guilt for having succumbed to the devil's alluring temptations. Satan uses that shame to make us feel we are unworthy of God's love. If we sin, we are terrible and that "terrible" person could not be accepted by a perfect God. The evil spirit gleefully informs us we have no backbone and will inevitably fall into more serious offences. Surely God can't forgive our repeated missteps the devil whispers softly in our ears. If he is right we should feel condemned to sin and sin again.

But God also encourages us to desire pleasure. We should pursue joy and happiness from nature, praising God, participating in and sharing our gifts and talents with others, and by celebrating the successes of friends and relatives. These cheerful situations and experiences are healthy and life-giving, unlike the amusements offered by the devil.

God encourages us to be sorry for our sins, acknowledge our failures, plead for his help and forgiveness, and then try not to repeat the sin. We participate in remorse not guilt. Committing sin does not motivate God to withdraw his generous love and graces from us because he cherishes us and will continue to assist and encourage us to live a wonderful Christian life. God has already forgiven our sins (past, present, and future) and prompts us to learn from our sin, repent and move on rather than wallow in shame and guilt. The option is ours: repentance and rebirth from God or sin and death from the evil one.

"But if a wicked man turns away from all the sins he has committed and keeps all my decrees and does what is just and right, he will surely live; he will not die. None of the offenses he has committed will be remembered against him. Because of the righteous things he has done, he will live." Ezekiel 18:21–22

The Power of Love

When the power of love overcomes the love of power, we will have peace. Jimi Hendrix

This is true in our own lives. When the power of love overcomes our wants and desires and we give control of our existence over to our God, our lives will become manageable. In fact, our lives will be extremely manageable. When we share and serve others, our wants and desires become less important, yet they are still met. Why do we waste our time trying to control everything (love of power), when our happiness and wellbeing depends on giving up our power and concentrating on loving others? Peace and serenity will come when we acknowledge our powerlessness, seek God, turn our cares over to God and implore his help in removing our shortcomings. People in twelve step programs like Alcoholics Anonymous or Gamblers' Anonymous are encouraged to surrender to God and allow him to remove their shortcomings so they can develop a better way of life. Peace and serenity can be theirs if they follow steps 1,2,3,6 and 7 by surrendering the love of power to the power of love.

Blessed be the God and Father of our Lord Jesus Christ. According to His great mercy, He has given us a new birth into a living hope through the resurrection of Jesus Christ from the dead, and into an inheritance that is imperishable, uncorrupted, and unfading, kept in heaven for you, who are being protected by God's power through faith for a salvation that is ready to be revealed in the last time. 1 Peter 1:3–5

"I will restore you to health and heal your wounds," declares the Lord. Jeremiah 30:17

Do not be wise in your own eyes; fear the Lord and shun evil. This will bring health to your body and nourishment to your bones. Proverbs 3:7–8

I keep the Lord in mind always because he is my right hand. I will not be shaken. Therefore my heart is glad, and my spirit rejoices; my body also rests securely. For you will not abandon me to Sheol; you will not allow your Faithful One to see the pit. You reveal the path of life to me; in your presence is abundant joy; in your right hand are eternal pleasures. Psalm 16:8–11

Now may the God of hope fill you with all joy and peace in believing, so that you may overflow with hope by the power of the Holy Spirit. Romans 15:13

We pray this in order that you may live a life worthy of the Lord and may please him in every way: bearing fruit in every good work, growing in the knowledge of God. Colossians 1:10

I am the Lord, your God, who takes hold of your right hand and says to you, Do not fear; I will help you. Isaiah 41:13

Praise God

The trumpeters and singers joined in unison, as with one voice, to give praise and thanks to the Lord. Accompanied by trumpets, cymbals and other instruments, they raised their voices in praise to the Lord and sang: "He is good; his love endures forever." Then the temple of the Lord was filled with a cloud, and the priests could not perform their service because of the cloud, for the glory of the Lord filled the temple of God. 2 Chronicles 5:13, 14

You are worthy, our Lord and God, to receive glory and honor and power, for you created all things, and by your will they were created and have their being. Revelation 4:11

Take time to thank God for his graciousness. Thank him for all the things you have received that you don't deserve. Be grateful you have not had trials that others have had. Rejoice in the knowledge that you are loved, cared for, and redeemed.

Preaching the Word

Example is the most effective preaching method we have. You might want to consider:

- Pray for someone in need
- Refuse to get angry over an injustice done to you
- Help out at the nursing home
- Encourage a suffering colleague
- Support someone who lost their spouse
- Go out of your way to assist a neighbor

If you have done any of the above actions you have done some wonderful preaching. Spreading the Good News, a form of preaching, can be done with the simplest of actions. It can be done at home, in the workplace, and on the street. Showing God's love is a way of proving to the world what and whom you believe in. Your manner of living demonstrates how the Gospel is working in you. You don't even have to say a word.

You need not be a missionary to Asia, Africa, or South America to be evangelizing the world. You can do it in your backyard. Living out the Gospel will speak volumes to your friends and neighbors and those to whom you come in contact on your life's journey. You need not be a Rhodes Scholar. Eloquent speaking is not a must. But a trusting heart and a compassionate being is necessary for you to preach God's words in the best way you know how (by being yourself and acting like a loving Christian).

Continue to pray for help and guidance from God. Receive the sacraments. Attend church. Be involved with some form of ministry. If you do, you can spread the Good News that we as Christians are called to do. St. Francis is supposed to have said that you should preach the Gospel and use words if necessary. You are able to do that. Pray, be yourself, and act in a Christian manner, and you will be following Jesus' command as told in the Gospel of Mark, "Go into all the world and preach the Good News to all creation."

Trust in the Lord with all your heart and lean not on your own understanding; in all your ways acknowledge him, and he will make your paths straight. Proverbs 3:5, 6

In everything I did, I showed you that by this kind of hard work we must help the weak, remembering the words the Lord Jesus himself said: 'It is more blessed to give than to receive.'" Acts 20:35

Let us not become weary in doing good, for at the proper time we will reap a harvest if we do not give up. Therefore, as we have opportunity, let us do good to all people, especially to those who belong to the family of believers. Galatians 6:9

Trust in the Lord and do good; dwell in the land and enjoy safe pasture. Delight yourself in the Lord and he will give you the desires of your heart. Commit your way to the Lord; trust in him and he will do this: Psalm 37:3–5

Make it your ambition to lead a quiet life, to mind your own business and to work with your hands, just as we told you, so that your daily life may win the respect of outsiders and so that you will not be dependent on anybody. 1 Thessalonians 4:11, 12

For I was hungry and you gave me something to eat, I was thirsty and you gave me something to drink, I was a stranger and you invited me in, I needed clothes and you clothed me, I was sick and you looked after me, I was in prison and you came to visit me." Then the righteous will answer him, "Lord, when did we see you hungry and feed you, or thirsty and give you something to drink? When did we see you a stranger and invite you in, or needing clothes and clothe you? When did we see you sick or in prison and go to visit you?" The King will reply, 'I tell you the truth, whatever you did for one of the least of these brothers of mine, you did for me." Matthew 25:35–40

Offer hospitality to one another without grumbling. Each one should use whatever gift he has received to serve others, faithfully administering God's grace in its various forms. 1 Peter 4:9, 10

Precious Elderly People

There is a joke that makes the point that old people, or the elderly, are valuable for such things as the gold in their teeth. The joke may be funny, but it certainly misses the real point that the elderly are valuable for many reasons, including knowledge, compassion, and guidance.

The elderly can be a wealth of **knowledge.** They have seen many things, experienced many situations, interacted with a myriad people, and provided solutions to numerous problems. They have a background that can be useful. Financial **Help and guidance** can usually be gleaned from the elderly. They have completed their career and have been able to invest money over a long period of time. They know how to make good business decisions and where to put your money for optimum growth. They have often been the local bank for their children and other relatives, usually providing interest-free loans. They may have even opened their home to visitors until they can be on their own.

Young people should tap in to this valuable resource. They might ask the elderly how to deal with a particular person or group of people. Many elderly can give great advice on investments and spending. From cars to homes, the elderly can provide advice that can save the young person time and money.

The elderly have a great capacity for **compassion and understanding.** They have experienced life and death. They have provided comfort and healing for the sick. They know the trials and tribulations of life. That experience gives them a unique vantage point from which they can provide comfort and support to the hurting individual. They also know how to appreciate the joys of life. They have experienced the birth of children, their youth, their marriage, and their celebrations and they know how to rejoice in the simple things in life. They live for the moment and expect God worry about their future.

More important than their help and guidance, compassion and understanding, and their knowledge is their **faith in God** and their willingness to do his will. Their example of faith can be a witness to children, neighbors, and acquaintances. Often children express the hope that they can be half as good as their parents or grandparents. Those elderly people have learned that God is the rock on which they can lean. He provides comfort, guidance, sustenance, and support to the many trials that people face in their lives. God, unlike people, will never let us down and will *always* be available in times of need. A spouse may become incapacitated or die, but God will be your constant companion in this life and the next. Faith in God is much more valuable than any earthly wisdom and a tremendous example the elderly can pass on to the young.

Truly the elderly are precious for all the above reasons. They are valuable as examples of faith and being children of God. Knowing this, we should value the elderly, treat them with respect, and give them a place of honor in our hearts. They should be acknowledged for the jewel that they have become. They have provided us with a blueprint on how to live life, help one another and be true to our God.

We will not hide them from their children; we will tell the next generation the praiseworthy deeds of the Lord, his power, and the wonders he has done. He decreed statutes for Jacob and established the law in Israel, which he commanded our forefathers to teach their children, so the next generation would know them, even the children yet to be born, and they in turn would tell their children. Then they would put their trust in God and would not forget his deeds but would keep his commands. Psalm 78:4–7

Command those who are rich in this present world not to be arrogant nor to put their hope in wealth, which is so uncertain, but to put their hope in God, who richly provides us with everything for our enjoyment. Command them to do good, to be rich in good deeds, and to be generous and willing to share. In this way they will lay up treasure for themselves as a firm foundation for the coming age, so that they may take hold of the life that is truly life. 1 Timothy 6:17–19

Therefore, as God's chosen people, holy and dearly loved, clothe yourselves with compassion, kindness, humility, gentleness and patience. Bear with each other and forgive whatever grievances you may have against one another. Forgive as the Lord forgave you. Colossians 3:12–13

Be devoted to one another in brotherly love. Honor one another above yourselves. Never be lacking in zeal, but keep your spiritual fervor, serving the Lord. Romans 12:10

A generous man will prosper; he who refreshes others will himself be refreshed. Proverbs 11:25

Precious Gifts

There is a story about a great king who invited the people to his castle each week to ask questions, seek help, or just complain. Each and every week a simply attired old man came to the court, not saying a word, and offered the king a large piece of fruit. The king graciously accepted the fruit, and the man left. The king didn't know what to do with the fruit, so he threw it out onto the garbage pile.

This procedure happened each and every week for a year, yielding no words from the man. One time the king gave the fruit to his pet monkey just after the man left. When the monkey started eating the fruit, he bit into something hard. The king noticed the monkey's dilemma and looked closely at the fruit. Inside the fruit was a precious jewel. The king then ordered his servants to check the garbage pile. Lo and behold, after picking through the pile they found a jewel in every piece of fruit the elderly man had brought.

The moral? We often don't recognize the real gifts people give us because we look at the outside wrapping and don't bother to delve deeper. The gift may seem insignificant, but may turn out to be a hidden jewel. We have to critically observe t the gifts we receive to see their true value.

Isn't that like our God? He provides spectacular gems hidden in the ordinary. We often overlook the precious gift (in whatever form) disguised inside because we only examine the exterior. So take time today to appreciate the prolific treasures God has given you. Look deeper into the ordinary things that happen in your life (the precious "thank you," the awesome note of encouragement, the friendly shoulder to leave your burdens on, and many, many more). Be observant and open to the hidden jewels God is sending your way this year.

Because of the Lord's great love we are not consumed, for his compassions never fail. They are new every morning; great is your faithfulness. The Lord is good to those whose hope is in him, to the one who seeks him. Lamentations 3:22–23, 25

Psalm 2011

God of creation:
>
> The earth reminds me of your greatness.
> Shows me again your creativity
> And astounds me with your brilliance.

When I see your earthly panorama:
>
> I praise You God of mountain vistas.
> I thank you for saguaro, ocotillo and prickly pear.
> I appreciate desert life sustained and nourished by your hand.

When monsoons reign down:
>
> I marvel at your power.
> I believe in your majesty.
> I trust your love will renew and enliven my soul.

When your sunsets greet my eyes:
>
> I am astounded at their greatness.
> I am enveloped by your spectacle of light and color.
> I sense you ever at my side.

All around me are signs of You, O Lord:
>
> Rainbows of vibrant colors and hues,
> People of faith, energy and kindness,
> Nourishment deliciously found in your word and sacraments.

All life is a testament to your magnificence.

Honor and tribute to you for morning newness, noon repasts, and long quiet evenings.

All day long my praises ascend upward to you.

May my awe and wonder of you be constant today and all the days I exist.

Tom

Pumpkins

A lady recently being baptized was asked by a coworker what it was like to be a Christian. She replied, "It's like being a pumpkin. God picks you from the patch, brings you in, and washes all the dirt off you. Then he cuts the top off and scoops out all the yucky stuff. He removes the seeds of doubt, hate, greed, etc., and then he carves you a new smiling face and puts his light inside of you to shine for all the world to see."

Wow! It that great or what? We are new creations after baptism, pure and free. We have the light of Christ in us encouraging us to grow and develop in grace and wisdom. We have the opportunity to share that light with those around us and be "Christ" to other people.

Don't let that opportunity go unused. Celebrate your baptism. Share your joy with others. Endeavor to spread the Good News to everyone you encounter. Be yourself, and allow God to let his light shine through you.

When Jesus spoke again to the people, he said, "I am the light of the world. Whoever follows me will never walk in darkness, but will have the light of life." John 8:12

For God, who said, "Let light shine out of darkness," made his light shine in our hearts to give us the light of the knowledge of the glory of God in the face of Christ. 2 Corinthians 4:6

No one lights a lamp and hides it in a jar or puts it under a bed. Instead, he puts it on a stand, so that those who come in can see the light. Luke 8:16

Remember This

God won't ask the square footage of your house, but he'll ask how many people you welcomed into your home.

God won't ask about the clothes you had in your closet, but he'll ask how many you helped to clothe.

God won't ask what your job title was, but he'll ask if you compromised your character to obtain it.

God won't ask how many friends you had, but he'll ask how many people to whom you were a friend.

God won't ask in what neighborhood you lived, but he'll ask how you treated your neighbors.

God won't ask about the color of your skin, but he'll ask about the content of your character.

God won't ask why it took you so long to seek Salvation, but He'll lovingly take you to your mansion in heaven, and not to the gates of Hell.

All of these comments off the internet remind us that God is love and we are called to love because God loved us first. Life is simple:

cherish your neighbors, pray for your friends, love your enemies and adore your God.

This is love: not that we loved God, but that he loved us and sent his Son as an atoning sacrifice for our sins. Dear friends, since God so loved us, we also ought to love one another. 1 John 4:10, 11

Right Where We Are

Thank you, Lord, for giving us _____. The phrase from this song, Right Where We Are, written by Pierre Tubbs and J. Vincent Edwards, are about being thankful. The blank could be filled with words such as: life, health, friends, church, or us. The point is to appreciate God for all the good things he has given us. Too often we take all the wonderful situations in our life for granted.

The verses of the song remind us that we should be thankful for _____ right where we are. That means we should enjoy ourselves no matter the situation. It is impressive when we see people who have lost loved ones being cheerful and encouraging. People who have lost jobs but have confidence in the Lord are inspiring. People who must relocate away from relatives and friends but can see much good in the situation are motivating to us. They all can enjoy the gifts from God they are receiving right where they are.

Too often we look ahead to changes and expect to be grateful for them. Why can't we enjoy the situation as it is unfolding? We need to look for the good in any situation, appreciating what we have, and not worrying about what we don't have. It means relying on God to provide for our needs, putting everything we have into our present situation. Don't worry about the past or the future. Both are in God's hands. Concentrate on the here and now, and let God take care of you. Happiness is all around us. Savor and enjoy it now.

Are not two sparrows sold for a penny? Yet not one of them will fall to the ground apart from the will of your Father. And even the very hairs of your head are all numbered. So don't be afraid; you are worth more than many sparrows. Matthew 10:29–31

Rocks

Rocks can be hard or smooth, hot or cold. They can be treacherous to climb and difficult to go around. But when they are crushed and mixed with the remains of animals and plants, they become rich soil that can produce beautiful flowers, tall trees, and an abundance of food in numerous varieties.

That is the way we are in life: rough or smooth, hot or cold, but not productive. When we allow God to fully enter our lives, we become rich soil, ready to develop and grow and become productive. It is our choice—stay barren and lifeless or become rich and fertile.

For he satisfies the thirsty and fills the hungry with good things. Psalm 107:9

Then Jesus declared, "I am the bread of life. He who comes to me will never go hungry, and he who believes in me will never be thirsty." John 6:35

And if you spend yourselves in behalf of the hungry and satisfy the needs of the oppressed, then your light will rise in the darkness, and your night will become like the noonday. The Lord will guide you always; he will satisfy your needs in a sun-scorched land and will strengthen your frame. You will be like a well-watered garden, like a spring whose waters never fail. Isaiah 58:10, 11

Small Things?

Do small things with great love. Mother Theresa

Give your child a big hug in the morning. Take out the garbage. Do your job diligently Comfort an ailing relative. Listen carefully to complaints of your spouse. All of these situations happen to us in our ordinary lives. The trick is to perform the ordinary tasks you have to do with great love. We all have common tasks to perform that we can accomplish while complaining, or we can do them with all the love we can muster. It is up to us.

God asks us to love him and show his love to others. We do that in our day-to-day living. We do that when we seek God and ask him to be with us during our normal activities. The more we seek God's help and let him support and guide us, the easier it is to live with a loving attitude.

Take time to look at your routine. Where can you include God? Where could you be more loving? How can you do your daily tasks with a Christian attitude? Seek God's help so you will grow in love in your service to God and your service to others.

A new command I give you: Love one another. As I have loved you, so you must love one another. By this all men will know that you are my disciples, if you love one another. John 13:34, 35

Stuffed

Have you ever eaten a little more than you should have at Thanksgiving? OK, maybe you consumed a great deal more than was comfortable. It was so much you felt that not a single grain of food could discover any hiding space in your stomach. You were so full no liquid could find a crevice to hide in or even slide down inside you. You were stuffed!

Being stuffed can be wonderful if it is with the right substance. Have you filled yourself with the energy from the sacraments? Are you bursting at the seams with calories from the Holy Spirit? Have you become so full of the Word of God that your being cannot absorb any more? Are your mind and your body completely soaked with the Good News of God's love for humankind? Are you so saturated with the thoughts of Jesus and his message that not a single crack is open to let anything else seep into?

You might have said "probably not" to all of these questions. But wouldn't it be great? The wonderfulness of God and his message would fill you up to almost bursting. You would feel compelled to praise God and do everything you could to show the world you are a believer.

We are imperfect beings, sinners and unworthy of grace or forgiveness. But God has been so generous Jesus was sent to make us imperfect beings worthy of God's love. We became heirs to his kingdom. With that in mind, we need to make every effort to put God as the center of our lives. He needs to come first. We must read his word, receive God's sacraments and aspire to live the way Jesus demonstrated for us in the New Testament. Every part of our being requires stuffing with God's love and forgiveness.

How are you going to become stuffed? When are you going to begin? How will you keep up your momentum when trials come your way? How will you set up God as your number one priority?

Overeating will make you feel bloated and uncomfortable. Being stuffed with God will energize and sustain you in this life. Be sure to allow God to satiate your body and soul with his aid, assurance, courage and fortitude in following the path he has designed for you. Don't wait until Thanksgiving to become stuffed with the message and graces of God.

Show me your ways, O Lord teach me your paths; guide me in your truth and teach me, for you are God my Savior, and my hope is in you all day long. Psalm 25:4, 5

Surprise

You quietly walked toward your child's bedroom. In the doorway you saw her in silent prayer, hands folded, eyes toward heaven, and a glow on her face. Surprise! You have just seen a glimpse of Jesus.

As you were leaving the auditorium having just watched Altar Boyz perform, you observed a wife and another elderly person trying to help a wheelchair-bound man gain his balance in his attempt to stand up and proceed to his motorized walker. Surprise! You have seen good Shepherd in action.

On Sunday, as you walked into church early, you noticed a young man deep in prayer. He looked so serene, so calm and saintly. Surprise! You have witnessed Jesus communicating with his father right in the God's own house.

Where, in your ordinary day, will you come face to face with Jesus? If God can be seen in the ordinary, then he must be visible to us many times during our day. He might be seen in our spouse, our child, our coworker, or ourselves when we look into the mirror. Whenever we see kindness, whenever we see holiness, whenever we see justice being done, we have had a glimpse of the Divine in our midst. And if we have seen Jesus, we have seen the father.

Do not be blinded by your preconceptions of what God is like as the Pharisees were or the people of Nazareth were. They expected a powerful earthly king and therefore could not accept Jesus as their Lord and Messiah because he didn't fit the picture of what they were expecting. Do not limit where God can do his work and by whom that work is completed. Let your eyes and ears be open to the possibility of God in the ordinary moments of your life. Using your senses be ready to be surprised and astounded.

But if from there you seek the Lord your God, you will find him if you look for him with all your heart and with all your soul. Deuteronomy 4:29

Know the love of Christ which surpasses knowledge, so that you may be filled up to all the fullness of God. Ephesians 3:19

Thanks to Deacon Al of St. Elizabeth Ann Seton Church because his homily was the impetus for this meditation.

Ten Commandments Part II

I. Thou shall spend time daily with your God in prayer.
II. Thou shall look for your God's face in the eyes of the lowly.
III. Thou shall seek your God's advice in all your actions.
IV. Thou shall help thy neighbor whenever possible.
V. Thou shall be a good servant to your earthy realm.
VI. Thou shall be generous in support of God's house of worship.
VII. Thou shall give thanks for the many blessings your God has provided.
VIII. Thou shall be open to the Holy Spirit's call.
IX. Thou shall have special concern for the welfare of God's children.
X. Thou shall be content with the gifts and talents God has given you.

We have been created with many wonderful gifts and talents that we are meant to share them with others. We need to constantly unearth ways to spread our numerous blessings to improve the lives of others less fortunate. It may be a matter of looking for things we should do rather than concentrating on things we shouldn't do.

We know God wants us to follow his commandments. But the Ten Commandments are only meant to be a minimum, a starting point in our relationship with our God and our fellow human beings. God wants us to seek ways to expand his love in us, and in turn, distribute that love with all those we meet. It is a love which is dynamic, creative, inventive and all inclusive.

Maybe we could enlarge our vision of God's love by creating a second set of commandments that concentrate on positive ways to interact with others in our daily life. These creative and all-inclusive commandments should be a method to enhance our ability to live and love as Jesus did. We would work diligently to improve our own way of treating the earth and its people in a manner pleasing to the father.

Once we have spent time creating our new commandments, we should devise ways to implement them and bring our concepts and ideas into real action. Continued consultation with God will help provide the energy we need to push our actions forward.

Once we feel we are doing well with our new set of commandments, we should go back and reevaluate them. Are we following them? Have our daily actions been more beneficial to others? Have we been better examples of Christian love? Where can we improve? What changes in our actions will bring them in harmony with our commandments?

These positive commandments would be a wonderful vehicle for us to dynamically change our relationships with ourselves, with our neighbors, with our earth, and especially with our God. Now is a great time to being your effort on creating your own Ten Commandments Part II.

Do nothing out of selfishness or out of vain glory; rather, humbly regard others as more important than yourselves, each looking out not for his own interests, but (also) everyone for those of others. Have among yourselves the same attitude that is also yours in Christ Jesus. Philippians 2:3–5

So I declare and testify in the Lord that you must no longer live as the Gentiles do, in the futility of their minds; darkened in understanding, alienated from the life of God because of their ignorance, because of their hardness of heart, they have become callous and have handed themselves over to licentiousness for the practice of every kind of impurity to excess. That is not how you learned

Christ, assuming that you have heard of him and were taught in him, as truth is in Jesus, that you should put away the old self of your former way of life, corrupted through deceitful desires, and be renewed in the spirit of your minds, and put on the new self, created in God's way in righteousness and holiness of truth. Ephesians 4:17–24

And whatever you do, in word or in deed, do everything in the name of the Lord Jesus, giving thanks to God the Father through him. Colossians 3:17

A good name is more desirable than great riches, and high esteem, than gold and silver. The kindly man will be blessed, for he gives of his sustenance to the poor. Proverbs 22:1, 9

Tell the rich in the present age not to be proud and not to rely on so uncertain a thing as wealth but rather on God, who richly provides us with all things for our enjoyment. Tell them to do good, to be rich in good works, to be generous, ready to share, thus accumulating as treasure a good foundation for the future, so as to win the life that is true life. 1 Timothy 6:17

That's All I Ask of You

In *The Phantom of the Opera*, Christine is troubled by the music of the night composed by the Phantom. The Phantom promises her beautiful music and a terrific voice to sing that music. All Christine has to do is love the Phantom.

Raoul, the hero, informs Christine that she doesn't have to be in the grips of the Phantom. He promises to love and guide her, protect her and be beside her. He and the daylight will give her freedom.

We can compare the characters in the play to God, the devil and us. God, like Raoul in the play, promises to love and guide us, protect us from evil, show us the light, and give us the freedom to be ourselves. All we have to do in return is love and adore God.

I will lead the blind by ways they have not know, along unfamiliar paths I will guide them: I will turn the darkness into light before them and make the rough places smooth. These are the things I will do; I will not forsake them. Isaiah 42:16

Raoul tells Christine, "I'm here. Nothing can harm you. My words will warm and calm you." God, through his words and actions, will provide us with warmth and calmness.

I will establish peace in the land that you may lie down to rest without anxiety. I will rid the country of ravenous beasts, and keep the sword of war from sweeping across your land. Leviticus 26:6

My people will live in peaceful country, in secure dwellings and quiet resting places. Isaiah 32:18

On the other hand, the Phantom, like the devil, only wants darkness and to be in control. There is no freedom when under the influence of the evil one.

Be sober and vigilant. Your opponent the devil is prowling around like a roaring lion looking for (someone) to devour. Resist him, steadfast in faith, knowing that your fellow believers throughout the world undergo the same sufferings. 1 Peter 5:8, 9

Nothing good can come out of being under the control of the evil one. The wicked shall be turned into hell, and all the nations that forget God. Psalm 9:17

Christine represents all of us who are tempted by the devil and the deceptions of the world. We need to make a decision: pursue and emulate God or follow the devil. Christine decides to follow Raoul (God) when she says, "Say you'll share with me one love, one lifetime. Say the word, and I will follow you. Love me. That's all I ask of you."

God does love us and promises us salvation if we accept him as Lord.

"The word is near you, in your mouth and in your heart" (that is, the word of faith that we preach), for, if you confess with your mouth that Jesus is Lord and believe in your heart that God raised him from the dead, you will be saved. Romans 10:9

Raoul expresses his love when he tells Christine, "Let me be your shelter; let me be your light. You're safe. No one will find you. Your fears are all behind you." Later he states, "Then say you'll share with me one love, one lifetime. Let me lead you from your solitude." God's word proclaims that he will graciously provide his all-encompassing love and abundant graces for us.

Now this is the message that we have heard from him and proclaim to you: God is light, and in him there is no darkness at all. If we say, "We have fellowship with him," while we continue to walk in darkness, we lie and do not act in truth. But if we walk in the light as he is in the light, then we have fellowship with one another, and the blood of his Son Jesus cleanses us from all sin. 1 John 1:5–7.

Our life is not a play; it is real. We will have consequences for our choices. So it is extremely important to make the right decisions. We must choose God to be children of the light and not be controlled by darkness and evil. The choice is ours: life or death, darkness or light, God or the devil. The options we take will affect our eternity. We know we can make the correct decisions because our God, our guide, our protector and constant companion, is always at our side providing just what we require. That's all we can ask from him

Be brave and steadfast; have no fear or dread of them, for it is the Lord, your God, who marches with you; he will never fail you or forsake you." Deuteronomy 31:6

That's God

When you get a sudden urge to do something nice for a person you love it might be a message from God who communicates to us through the Holy Spirit.

This paraphrased message from the internet should be a reminder to us that God does work in this world. He is not just a person who lived two thousand years ago. God is living in today's world. He is alive and well and dwelling in your heart. Listen to him.

Pay attention to that little voice that encourages you to reach out and provide assistance to one of God's children. Be open to the suggestions God sends your way. Be still and know your God.

Read God's words in the Bible. Receive his sacraments. Associate with his followers. Practice God's instructions to love one another incorporating his message into your life.

You cannot effectively listen to God without building a relationship with him. Talk to him in prayer, and let God motivate you to be a messenger of his care and concern for the people on earth. Keep the lines of communication open. Be ready to accept his call and follow through with concrete actions.

But God demonstrates his own love for us in this: While we were still sinners, Christ dies for us. Romans 5:8

The Lord said, "Go out and stand on the mountain in the presence of the Lord, for the Lord is about to pass by."

Then a great and powerful wind tore the mountains apart and shattered the rocks before the Lord, but the Lord was not in the wind. After the wind there was an earthquake, but the Lord was not in the earthquake. After the earthquake came a fire, but the Lord was not in the fire. And after the fire came a gentle whisper. When Elijah heart it, he pulled his cloak over his face and went out and stood at the mouth of the cave. 1 Kings 19:11-13

Three Little Pigs

Is our life like the story of the three little pigs? If we believe in God and say that we are Christian but don't do anything to strengthen our faith, then we are like the first little pig whose house was made of straw. We imagine our own wisdom and fortitude will take care of us in times of trouble. But some tragedy occurs that challenges us to our very soul, and then we find out our straw house is no match for the problem. The wolf, whether it be in the form of a business setback, accident, or death in the family, easily blows down our straw house. We fall to pieces, not knowing what direction to go or what to do. We may even curse God for our own misfortune. Where was God when we needed him?

We might be a little better off than the first pig if we attend church regularly. We would be like the pig whose house is made of sticks. Our house of sticks looks strong, but it cannot withstand a strong attack on our faith. When tragedy and sorrow enters our lives, we are not equipped to handle it. We succumb to the situation and begin to blame others for our misery. Or we might sit on the pity pot, complaining about how unfair life is. Even though we have attended church, our faith has not been nourished enough to cope with the challenges that life has to offer us. Our house of sticks crumbles around us.

We should be like that last little pig whose house is made of brick. Not only do we attend church regularly (sometimes not even on Sunday), we receive the sacraments and read the word of God daily and associate with friends of strong faith. When a situation comes to challenge us, we have all the tools we need to overcome the problem. We don't despair because we know that God is ready, willing, and able to get us through and beyond our trials. The problems don't become easier, but our attitude toward them enables us to put the difficulty in perspective. We can see a solution or can accept those problems that are ongoing. Our strong faith in God encourages us to anticipate a rising from our problems either in this world or the next.

Take time to examine your house. What is it made of? Can it withstand the wolf at your door? Are your tools up to the challenge? What can you do to improve your structure and foundation? When you close the door to your house at night and you are inside, will you feel apprehensive or confident?

The grass withers and the flowers fall, but the word of our God stands forever." Isaiah 40:8

But the Lord is faithful; he will strengthen you and guard you from the evil one.2 Thessalonians 3:3

Too Much?

Too much happiness in a person is like too much cotton candy—sugary, sticky, and a little nauseating. Whereas joy is like a hot air balloon, for it lifts all who enter it, it buoys the spirit, and it offers a higher perspective. Patsy Clairmont

So aren't you glad you have some times in your life that are less than wonderful? Probably not. But the statement above does remind us that there are tough times in everybody's life. Life is not fair, equal, or presented to us in nice even patters. It is chaotic, unpredictable and sometimes overwhelming. It also has the possibility of being terrific.

It all depends on us and our outlook. We know that God loves us and will protect us. He will get us through those tough times. God will also be there to celebrate with us during times of joy. He is in the midst us in *all* our times: tough, boring, average, and extraordinary. Since we have free will, we can invite God to participate with us in our daily activities or just when times are difficult. It is our call: have God with us part time or full time; there to help only in times of trouble, or to join us fully in all facets of our life.

May the God of hope fill you with all joy and peace as you trust in him, so that you may overflow with hope by the power of the Holy Spirit. Romans 15:13

TYSM

One of the latest things people have put on their e-mails is TYSM which stands for *thank you so much*. It is a nice sentiment, but like many things today, we use it to rush through our thoughts and try to put them into the shortest and easiest method to save our time and energy. We don't have to spend time thinking about what we write or say. We simply put down the letters, and we are done. Simple, easy, and thoughtless.

Is that that way we treat God and all his blessings? Do we appreciate his abundance with just a simple thank you and then rush about our daily lives? Do we bother to humbly thank the Lord for his generosity in the morning and the evening and other times during the day? Is a grateful thank you even in our prayers? Do we go right to the petitions that we feel are so important in our lives?

Maybe we need to stop, slow down, and ponder the many opportunities and gifts God has provided us on a daily basis. Are we grateful for the healthy child born into our family but guilty of not recalling that not all children are born without problems?

In all circumstances give thanks, for this is the will of God for you in Christ Jesus. 1 Thessalonians 5:18

Do we spend time thanking God for the gift of recovery after a serious illness? Do we realize that recovery is not always the result? Have we taken time to appreciate the skill and dedication God has given to the surgeons who have helped to make our recovery possible?

The Lord is my strength and my shield, in whom my heart trusted and found help. So my heart rejoices; with my song I praise my God. Psalm 28:7

What about your job? Are you grateful you have one and do not have to rely on the St. Vincent DePaul Society or the local food bank for your next meal? Imagine the stress and anxiety you avoid by not having to beg for food or for money to pay your electric bill. Think about the shame you would feel if you had to rely on others to meet your family needs.

Shout joyfully to the Lord, all you lands; worship the Lord with cries of gladness; come before him with joyful song. Know that the Lord is God, our maker to whom we belong, whose people we are, God's well-tended flock. Enter the temple gates with praise, its courts with thanksgiving. Give thanks to God, bless his name; good indeed is the Lord, whose love endures forever, whose faithfulness lasts through every age. Psalm 100

TYSM is short, simple, and in many cases used without thought. Make sure your thankfulness is well thought out and from the heart, not hurried or delivered with a cavalier attitude. You have many things to be grateful for; just look around you. Then begin to express your appreciation to the Lord.

Therefore, we who are receiving the unshakable kingdom should have gratitude, with which we should offer worship pleasing to God in reverence and awe. Hebrews 12:28

We Don't Need Christians

We don't need more Christians. We need more people who demonstrate they are Christians by their actions. St. Francis said we should preach the Gospel and use words if necessary. Our actions do speak louder than our words. Make sure your actions demonstrate you are a devoted Christian and not a Christian in name only. Be sure your actions and life style reflect your beliefs.

In everything that he undertook in the service of God's temple and in obedience to the law and the commands, he sought his God and worked wholeheartedly. And so he prospered. 2 Chronicles 31:21

Even a child is known by his actions, by whether his conduct is pure and right. Proverbs 20:11

God is not unjust; he will not forget your work and the love you have shown him as you have helped his people and continue to help them. We want each of you to show this same diligence to the very end, in order to make your hope sure. Hebrews 6:10, 11

When I'm...

Lord,

When I'm cross and irritable, let me realize you suffered for my sins so I may relinquish my petty irritations.

He himself bore our sins in his body on the tree, so that we might die to sins and live for righteousness; by his wounds you have been healed. 1 Peter 2:24

When I'm judgmental of others, let me see you on your cross where you asked the father to forgive your tormentors because they knew not what they were doing.

But he was pierced for our transgressions, he was crushed for our iniquities; the punishment that brought us peace was upon him, and by his wounds we are healed. Isaiah 53:5

When I'm in doubt, let me see your love in others so I may strengthen my faith in you.

Those who hope in the Lord will renew their strength. They will soar on wings like eagles; they will run and not grow weary, they will walk and not be faint. Isaiah 40:31

When I feel rejected by others, let me learn to forgive them and move on, leaving my guilt, anger, and blame behind me.

Get rid of all bitterness, rage and anger, brawling and slander, along with every form of malice. Be kind and compassionate to one another, forgiving each other, just as in Christ God forgave you. Be imitators of God, therefore, as dearly loved children. Ephesians 4:31–33

When I feel lonely, may I find your love in your sacraments and your church so I can really understand you are with me at all times.

Do not fear, for I am with you; do not be dismayed, for I am your God. I will strengthen you and help you; I will uphold you with my righteous right hand. Isaiah 41:10

When I am lazy, may other Christians remind me that I am your servant and need to actively work on your behalf to spread the Good News of your love and forgiveness for all people.

Then I realized that it is good and proper for a man to eat and drink, and to find satisfaction in his toilsome labor under the sun during the few days of life God has given him—for this is his lot. Moreover, when God gives any man wealth and possessions, and enables him to enjoy them, to accept his lot and be happy in his work—this is a gift of God. Ecclesiastes 5:18, 19

O gracious Lord, you know I am a sinner with many faults and weaknesses. Help me, through your word, sacraments, and church, to overcome those failings, and see my strengths and gifts which you have given me so I may use my talents in service to you. Amen.

What Was That Sign?

Janet's parents were nice. They ran a church camp in northern Wisconsin. On the way to the camp, Janet's dad had a tendency to drive very quickly His wife never said to slow down or told him that he was going too fast. She simply looked out the side window, moved her head quickly from front to back, and said "What was that sign?" Janet's dad understood the implication and began to slow down.

Are we driving too fast? Are we not slowing down when we need to? Are we spending as much time as we can on things that are important? Do we speed too fast to read the signs along the way?

A particular place where we tend to speed rapidly is in our relationship with God. Do we give God a quick nod by giving him an hour of our time one day each week? Are we so quick with our meal prayers that we don't pay attention to the words? Do we recite the words out of habit? Do we even stop long enough to say meaningful opening and closing prayers of our day.

God wants us to appreciate the fact that he is the most essential person in our lives. We need to slow down and communicate with God on a personal level. Our conversations (prayers) need to be thoughtful, meaningful, and sincere. They can't be sincere, thoughtful, or meaningful, if we rush through them.

What about our Liturgy? It can't have an impact in our lives if we don't concentrate on the event, become fully involved, and forget about outside concerns. The worship service needs to be the most important thing on our mind at that time. As difficult as it is, we need to be focused on God and what he wants us to digest from his words in the Liturgy.

A fantastic friendship takes time and effort. God should be out best friend. Spend quality time with him, revolving your day around God instead of God revolving around your day. Make a commitment today to slow down, to communicate with God, to save quality time for the one who created you, and to keep him in your mind at all times instead of once a week or only at designated prayer times. Be sure you are driving slow enough to read the signs God sends your way on the road of life. Don't be caught asking, "What was that sign?".

But be very careful to keep the commandment and the law that Moses the servant of the Lord gave you: to love the Lord your God, to walk in all his ways, to obey his commands, to hold fast to him and to serve him with all your heart and all your soul." Joshua 22:5

With, For, In

Children like to use little words, while adults use large and complicated words. Adults like to take pride in their intelligence. Instead of adults' words to describe God, such as majestic, justifiable, and omnipotent, what might we learn from childlike words such as: with, for and in.

God is with us. He promised to be at our side, to be our support and our guide. God will be all the protection we ever need.

Therefore go and make disciples of all nations, baptizing them in the name of the Father and of the son and of the Holy Spirit, and teaching them to obey everything I have commanded you. And surely I am with you always, to the very end of the age. Matthew 28:19–20

Even though I walk through the valley of the shadow of death, I will fear no evil, for you are with me; your rod and your staff, they comfort me. Isaiah 54:10

God is for us, on our side, in our corner, and loves us unconditionally.

"Though the mountains be shaken and the hills be removed, yet my unfailing love for you will not be shaken nor my covenant of peace be removed," says the Lord, who has compassion on you. Isaiah 54:10

"Because he loves me," says the Lord, "I will rescue him; I will protect him, for he acknowledges my name." Psalm 91:14

God is also in us. He is part of our being and will not be separated from us.

"I am the vine; you are the branches. If a man remains in me and I in him, he will bear much fruit; apart from me you can do nothing. If anyone does not remain in me, he is like a branch that is thrown away and withers; such branches are picked up, thrown into the fire and burned. If you remain in me and my words remain in you, ask whatever you wish, and it will be given you." John 15:5–7

On that day you will realize that I am in my father, and you are in me, and I am in you. John 14:20

The choice is ours. We can think and act like adults and be impressed with our intelligence, or we can be childlike and have faith that God is with us, for, and in us.

Your Love is Finer than Life

O God, I seek you, my soul thirsts for you, your love is finer than life. Marty Haugen

This Responsorial Psalm reminds us to ask ourselves if God is the center of our lives. God should be, but he tends to be put on the back burner with most of us. Our list of important people and things might look like this: my children, my spouse, my family, my friends, my job, my house, my God, my hobbies, my church.

It is not easy putting God in the center of our lives. Life becomes so busy we relegate God to one hour on Sunday and some special occasions like weddings, funerals, and first communions. We even tend to forget about our morning and evening prayers when life gets hectic. But that is not the way God wants it to be. So what do we do?

As humans being influenced by satan, we have trouble putting God first. The devil tries to influence us to ignore God. So that can be our first step. Pray to God that he will help us put him upper most in our lives. The more we pray, the more God will influence our decisions.

We should make an effort to rediscover God in our daily lives, in the ordinary things we do. The people we meet all have some aspect of God in them. We need to recognize their goodness and be thankful to God.

We need to thank God for showing us his face through theirs. We can continue to observe recognizing aspects of God in other people and in many situations.

One situation we can look at differently is our job. God is the source of our income and survival, not our job. We should be appreciative when the job goes well and should be comforted in knowing God will provide for us if we lose our job. We can be open to other job opportunities because we know God wants the best for us and will not leave us orphaned.

As we pray and search for God in the people we meet and the situations we encounter, the more God will rise in rank on our list. As he becomes more noteworthy to us, it will become easier to see God in more situations and people. He will continue to move up the ladder of importance in our lives.

Be prepared for setbacks because the devil is persistent. But God is also persistent. He will provide the influence and courage to move forward and continue to support us to change and grow. We will continue to develop until one day God will be on the top of our list where he belongs. We will then realize that God's love is finer than life itself.

Jesus replied: "'Love the Lord your God with all your heart and with all your soul and with all your mind.' This is the first and greatest commandment. And the second is like it: 'Love your neighbor as yourself.' Matthew 22:37–39

Section Five:
Acrostic Poetry

God has been very generous with us, providing us with many gifts and talents. We are uniquely and wonderfully made and are not exactly like anyone else in history. With these varied gifts, we can praise and acknowledge our God in many different ways. Acrostic poems provide us with the opportunity to express our gratitude to our God in short verses, deep with feeling and emotion. This same poetry can be a reminder of our need for God and the many ways we can access his support and blessings. Our joy and celebration can find nourishment and expression in acrostic poetry. Poetry can help soothe our soul and enlighten our minds and be a powerful means to give glory and praise to our God.

You will go out in joy and be led forth in peace; the mountains and hills will burst into song before you, and all the trees of the field will clap their hands. Isaiah 55:12

Light is shed upon the righteous and joy on the upright in heart. Rejoice in the Lord, you who are righteous, and praise his holy name. Psalm 97:11, 12

Nehemiah said, "Go and enjoy choice food and sweet drinks, and send some to those who have nothing prepared. This day is sacred to our Lord. Do not grieve, for the joy of the Lord is your strength." Nehemiah 8:10

I delight greatly in the Lord; my soul rejoices in my God. For he has clothed me with garments of salvation and arrayed me in a robe of righteousness, as a bridegroom adorns his head like a priest, and as a bride adorns herself with her jewels. Isaiah 61:10

BIBLE

Beautiful people
Inspired to read
Bible passages to
Learn about God's
Eternal plan

Did Jesus really love women? Read the Bible and find out. What were his feelings toward gentiles? Study the bible to learn. What about Jesus and the people on the fringe of society—the unclean, the poor and the lowly? The Bible is where the answers can be found.

God has a saving plan for you. He wants you to be with him in paradise. One way to understand and appreciate that fact is to take a Bible course. God communicates through the writers of the Gospels and other passages in the Bible. All you have to do is peruse the Bible, discuss the material, and put those concepts into practice.

It is a lifelong process, so don't wait until next month or next year to begin. The best time is now. You can read the Bible and study the commentaries to start with and then look for Bible study courses that you can use to build on your knowledge of God and his plan. The more you learn, the better you will understand God's love for you and his plan for your salvation. As you read and study, you will become inspired to understand even more.

Your word is a lamp to my feet and a light for my path. I delight in your decrees; I will not neglect your word. Do good to your servant, and I will live; I will obey your word. Psalm 119:105; 119:16, 17

In my Father's house are many rooms; if it were not so, I would have told you. I am going there to prepare a place for you. John 14:2, 3

To the Jews who had believed him, Jesus said, "If you hold to my teaching, you are really my disciples. Then you will know the truth, and the truth will set you free." John 8:31, 32

Continue daily to become one of the beautiful people eager to conceptualize and digest the contents and life giving principles of the Bible.

BIBLE #2

Basic
Instruction
Before
Leaving
Earth

Deacon Al, who works with the St. Elizabeth Ann Seton teens, stated that we are to read the Bible. The teens have been instructed that the letters in the word Bible mean: Basic Instructions Before Leaving Earth. What a great way to remember the importance of God's word as found in his holy book. But is this acronym really something we should take seriously in our daily lives?

The Bible covers many of the concerns we face in our personal lives. One concern might be the need for encouragement. Is God available to motivate us during our hectic days? From Lamentations we learn the answer.

This I call to mind and therefore I have hope: Because of the Lord's great love we are not consumed, for his compassions never fail. They are new every morning; great is your faithfulness. Lamentations 3:21–23

Is money something that should be very important in our lives? The Bible has many things to say about wealth.

Listen, my dear brothers: Has not God chosen those who are poor in the eyes of the world to be rich in faith and to inherit the kingdom he promised those who love him? James 2:5.

Wealth is also covered in Proverbs 22:2; Deuteronomy 8:18, 1 Timothy 6:17–19; and Ecclesiastes 4:6.

As children how are we to treat our parents?

Honor your father and your mother, as the Lord your God has commanded you, so that you may live long and that it may go well with you in the land the Lord your God is giving you. Deuteronomy 5:16

More information can be found in: Proverbs 23:22; 1 Timothy 5:4; Psalm 119:9 and Proverbs 6:20–22.

When we doubt ourselves and think we are worthless, we can turn to God's word and see how he feels about us.

The Lord appeared to us in the past, saying: "I have loved you with an everlasting love; I have drawn you with loving-kindness." Jeremiah 31:3

God reminds us in Isaiah that we are so important that he will never forget us.

Can a mother forget the baby at her breast and have no compassion on the child she has borne? Though she may forget, I will not forget you! See, I have engraved you on the palm of my hands; your walls are ever before me. Isaiah 49:15, 16

When we screw up in our lives, can we depend on God to look kindly on us?

Seek the Lord while he may be found; call on him while he is near. Let the wicked forsake his way and the evil man his thoughts. Let him turn to the Lord, and he will have mercy on him, and to our God, for he will freely pardon. Isaiah 55:6–7.

More examples of God's mercy can be found in the words of James 5:11; 1 Peter 1:3; Titus 3:5 and Lamentations 3:22–23.

Putting on the armor of God is one way we can use God's word to meet the challenges, conflicts, and difficulties of our days.

Put on the full armor of God so that you can take your stand against the devil's schemes. Ephesians 6:11.

Take the helmet of salvation and the sword of the spirit, which is the word of God. Ephesians 6:17.

For the word of God is living and active. Sharper than any double-edged sword, it penetrates even to dividing soul and spirit, joints and marrow; it judges the thoughts and attitudes of the heart. Hebrews 4:12

It is helpful to remember that God has told us we are his children and are destined to have eternal life with him in heaven.

For the wages of sin is death, but the gift of God is eternal life in Christ Jesus our Lord. Romans 6:23.

For God so loved the world that he gave his one and only son, that whoever believes in him shall not perish but have eternal life. John 3:16.

The world and its desires pass away, but the person who does the will of God lives forever. 1 John 2:17.

God's word as found in the Bible covers these topics and many more—more than enough to meet all our needs, desires, and concerns. Start today to become more familiar with the Bible. Study and use the concepts located within its pages. Remember the Bible is your Basic Instructions Before Leaving Earth, so enjoy, prosper, and be comforted by its words today and all the days of your life.

CAT

Cute, cuddly, curious, cunning
Attentive, attractive, absorbing
Tender, tame, temperamental

Are any of these description applicable to you as a Christian? Yes, you should be as curious as a cat. How? You should be terribly interested in discovering your God.

Who is he? What has he done for me? What is God's history? What is his goal for me? What should I accomplish, in God's name, in my lifetime? How best can I get to know my Lord and Savior?

Look to the cat. Observe its curious side. Use that inquisitiveness as a model in discerning God and his plan for you.

No sleeping on the job! Work diligently to refine or expand your catlike quality of curiosity today. Strive to understand and become friends with your almighty and powerful God.

And without faith it is impossible to please God, because anyone who comes to him must believe that he exists and that he rewards those who earnestly seek him. Hebrews 11: 6

Those who know your name will trust in you, for you, Lord, have never forsaken those who seek you. Psalm 9:10

But if from there you seek the Lord your God, you will find him if you look for him with all your heart and with all your soul. Deuteronomy 4:29

CHILD

Chosen by God
>We are not an accident.
>We were created on purpose and for a purpose.
>God knows each one of us by name.

Held in high esteem
>We are regarded as saints.
>We are heirs to God's kingdom.
>God has saved a special place for us.

Individual
>We are unique.
>In all the world there is no one exactly like us.
>God's infinite ability created us as a one-of-a-kind brilliant jewel.

Loved by God
>God sent his son to die for us.
>We are more precious than all of God's other creations.
>We are created in God's image.

Devoted to each other

    We need to care about each other's thoughts and feelings.

    We are all part of the Body of Christ.

    We need to treat each other as if we were Christ himself.

The Lord appeared to us in the past, saying: "I have loved you with an everlasting love; I have drawn you with loving-kindness." Jeremiah 31:3

CHRISTIAN

Charity   Canada

Heralds   Haiti

Religious   Romania

Individuals   Italy

Servants   Spain

Trusting   Trinidad

Inviting   Ireland

Active   Argentina

Nice   New Zealand

All are gathered together in the human condition to serve and worship our God, our Lord and Savior. It makes not a bit of difference that one if from Argentina while one is from Italy. Nor does it matter that one is from Haiti and its culture while one is from Canada in its unique but different culture. People are all united in their belief in one God, Creator of us all. All are united in a universal service to each other and to God. May we never forget our mission: to love and to serve and to trust in God and his love and mercy.

The Lord gives sight to the blind, the Lord lifts up those who are bowed down, the Lord loves the righteous. Psalm 146:8

The Lord, your God, is in your midst, a mighty savior; He will rejoice over you with gladness, and renew you in his love, He will sing joyfully because of you, as one sings at festivals. Zephaniah 3:17, 18

I love those who love me, and those who seek me find me. Proverbs 8:17

Grace to all who love our Lord Jesus Christ with an undying love. Ephesians 6:24

Crayons and Your ABC's

We could learn a lot from crayons. Some are sharp, some are pretty, some are dull, some have weird names, and all are different colors, but they all have to learn to live in the same box. Robert Fulghum

This quote is very appropriate for us today. We need to celebrate our differences and share our similarities. One is not more important than the other both acting in tandem to make life interesting, challenging, and peaceful.

We might look to little children to remind us how we adults should act. We should remember our ABC's.

> **Allow for mistakes (theirs and ours)**
> **Be a friend (in good times and bad)**
> **Count on God (the one constant in our lives)**

If we appreciate that we are just one shade in a rainbow of colors having differences that need not separate us from others we can accept miscues of others and our own to be a friend at all times. God will bring these many crayons together to create a tapestry of life for us that is exciting and worthwhile. It's as easy as ABC.

At that time Jesus said, "I praise you, Father, Lord of heaven and earth, because you have hidden these things from the wise and learned, and revealed them to little children. Matthew 11:25

Though the mountains be shaken and the hills be removed, yet my unfailing love for you will not be shaken nor my covenant of peace be remove," says the Lord, who has compassion on you. Isaiah 54:10

DESERT

Dry times in our life
Especially difficult to comprehend
Stunned to the core of our being
Expecting a miracle
Requesting God's intervention
Thankful for God's uplifting grace

Dry! Lifeless! We feel that way sometimes. It usually happens after a tragedy or if we are in the midst of a long and seemingly endless problem. We do not feel in control, but rather helpless and overwhelmed. We can't quite understand what's happening.

At those "desert times" in our life we find it difficult to pray much less be thankful to God. We want answers, solutions, and comfort.

During these extremely difficult circumstances, God is with us, gently encouraging and comforting. That encouragement and comfort may come from a relative or friend or it might be something we see, hear or read. We might assume they are all random situations, but in essence they all have the hand of God as their source. God will provide whatever people and events are needed to help lessen our uneasiness, pain, and suffering. We will not be left alone to solve our problems because God has promised never to abandon us.

After the situation has improved (and it will), our prayer life is up and running, and we have more confidence, we should look back at our situation and observe that God's gentle touch has been guiding and supporting us. Then we need to take time to offer our thanks to God for his faithfulness, care, concern, and generosity because we could not have overcome the problem without God's grace and guidance.

We are hard pressed on every side, but not crushed; perplexed, but not in despair; persecuted, but not abandoned; struck down, but not destroyed. 2 Corinthians 4:8, 9

Though I walk in the midst of trouble, you preserve my life; you stretch out your hand against the anger of my foes, with your right hand you save me. Psalm 138:7

Do not let your hearts be troubled. Trust in God; trust also in me. In my Father's house are many rooms; if it were not so, I would have told you. I am going there to prepare a place for you. And if I go and prepare a place for you, I will come back and take you to be with me that you also may be where I am." John 14:1–31

I will be glad and rejoice in your love, for you saw my affliction and knew the anguish of my soul. Psalm 31:7

I lift up my eyes to the hills—where does my help come from? My help comes from the Lord, the Maker of heaven and earth. He will not let your foot slip—he who watches over you will not slumber; indeed, he who watches over Israel will neither slumber nor sleep. The Lord watches over you—the Lord is your shade at your right hand; the sun will not harm you by day, nor the moon by night. The Lord will keep you from all harm—he will watch over your life; the Lord will watch over your coming and going both now and forevermore. Psalm 121:1–8

The ransomed of the Lord will return. They will enter Zion with singing; everlasting joy will crown their heads. Gladness and joy will overtake them, and sorrow and sighing will flee away. Isaiah 51:11

But the Lord is faithful, and he will strengthen and protect you from the evil one. 2 Thessalonians 3:3

FOOL

Faithful
Observer and follower
Of our gracious
Lord's word and example

The world, through the media, says to buy expensive clothes to feel good; clothes make the man. In order to show your love for your wife, you need to buy her diamonds. Going to the spa not only shows good taste, but it is relaxing before or after the battle to get ahead in the business world.

TV and movies highlight the world's view of life. Reality shows dictate how we should treat others. "What should I do to get the most of my relationship to benefit myself? What's in it for me?" Movies seem to validate sex as a wonderful tool to satisfy a person's needs and desires. After all, sex and love are the same thing, right? Violence is also seen in the media as a useful means to obtain justice. Retaliation should be the tool of choice instead of offering forgiveness.

Only a fool would not accept these worldly views. But that is what we are called to be, "Fools for Christ." We are instructed to be faithful to God's words as they are shown to us through Jesus Christ. That makes us a fool in the eyes of the world.

Unlike the worldly view, love is not sex. From the Bible we know that love is so much more than sex.

Love is patient, love is kind. It does not envy, it does not boast, it is not proud. It is not rude, it is not self-seeking, it is not easily angered, it keeps no record of wrongs. Love does not delight in evil but rejoices with the truth. It always protects, always trusts, always hopes, always perseveres. Love never fails. 1 Corinthians 13:4

Christ's view of life is not to see what we can do to satisfy our desires but instead to love and serve God.

So if you faithfully obey the commands I am giving you today—to love the Lord your God and to serve him with all your heart and with all your soul—then I will send rain on your land in its season, both autumn and spring rains, so that you may gather in your grain, new wine and oil. Deuteronomy 11:13–15

We are also here to serve others.

Love must be sincere. Hate what is evil; cling to what is good. Be devoted to one another in brotherly love. Honor one another above yourselves. Romans 12:9, 10

A "Fool for Christ" will also not believe all those ads that constantly encourage us to buy things to make us happy. We are not to worry about worldly things but concern ourselves with God's truths.

Do not be anxious about anything, but in everything, by prayer and petition, with thanksgiving, present your requests to God. And the peace of God, which transcends all understanding, will guard your hearts and your minds in Christ Jesus. Philippians 4:6, 7

Will it be easy to be a "Fool?" No! It will take substantial work. Your constant effort will require support from God through prayer and petition. Encouragement will also be gleaned from reading scripture, receiving the sacraments, and being active in church. These tools to survival in an ungodly world are available to all of us. We just need to take advantage of them to become the best fool possible

Everyone born of God overcomes the world. This is the victory that has overcome the world, even our faith. Who is it that overcomes the world? Only he who believes that Jesus is the Son of God. 1 John 5:4, 5

FROG

Forgetting our worries
Relying on God's strength
Over and over again
Grateful and relaxed in God's care

A frog is cute and seems rather helpless in the jungle. But the frog manages to survive.

When our life seems to be out of control, we need to remember the frog. God will protect us, lead us, and support us. We are not helpless because God loves us dearly. We need not despair. With God at our side, we can accept our difficulties and work through them. He will always provide a solution or acceptance to all our problems and concerns. We are required to put our anxieties in God's hands and relax praying to God for assistance in being open to his divine guidance.

So be a frog. Don't worry about the future because God has already been there and will provide whatever means necessary to satisfy our concerns. Being open to God's solutions means we accept God's will and do not put demands on him to solve the problem the way we think it should be done. God's insights and resolutions are always better than our own. Like the frog in the jungle we will not be without resources and protection.

Trust in the Lord and do good; dwell in the land and enjoy safe pasture. Delight yourself in the Lord and he will give you the desires of your heart. Commit your way to the Lord; trust in him and he will do this. Psalm 37:3–5

KITES

Keeping in mind God's
Interest in our well being
Today, tomorrow, here, there, and
Everywhere imaginable, feeling
Safe in His loving arms

The next time you see a kite soaring, fly a kite, or even think about a kite, remember that God loves you with an everlasting love. You are precious and belong to him. Be content and grateful. Soar in the knowledge of God's unconditional and abundant love for you.

The Lord appeared to us in the past, saying: "I have loved you with an everlasting love; I have drawn you with loving - kindness. Jeremiah 31:3

For this reason I kneel before the father, from whom every family in heaven and on earth is named, that he may grant you in accord with the riches of his glory to be strengthened with power through his Spirit in the inner self, and that Christ may dwell in your hearts through faith; that you, rooted and grounded in love, may have strength to comprehend with all the holy ones what is the breadth and length and height and depth, and to know the love of Christ that surpasses knowledge, so that you may be filled with all the fullness of God. Ephesians 3:14–19

Prayer

Praising God
Reading scripture
Active participant in life
You and God one on one
Eagerly communicating
Ready to learn and do

Praising God is easy. We do it in church often through song and prayer. It's good to remember that God is God and we are not. Praise God, the Creator, Counselor, Prince of Peace, and Good Shepherd.

Reading scripture can be part of our prayer life. First we must request God's help in putting us in the right frame of mind to learn from the readings. Then we peruse the scripture and spend quality time reflecting on the words we have read.

Prayer also happens when we participate fully in life. That means we add God to the mix acting as if God is physically at our side. We deal with life in a Christ-like manner embracing life instead of running away from it. We include God in determining our actions and reactions to our everyday situations.

Prayer is God and us. It is personal. It is real. It involves sharing our hopes, thoughts, and dreams with the one who formed us and made us who we are. It is a close relationship.

Communications is important in prayer. It conveys feelings, both negative and positive. Communication is discussing our failures, successes, and concerns asking for help, which allows for change in us. It is an appreciation for past blessings as well as a commitment to "stay in touch."

Prayer says we are ready to act. Once we have discovered what we should do according to God's will, we need the willingness to do just that— God's will. The more we pray to God, the more we are willing to put our efforts into his goals.

Prayer is all of these concepts and more. It is life giving, spiritual, calming, spontaneous, and variable. We pray in the manner needed depending on the situation and our feelings or moods. It can be adapted, rearranged, and changed so we can come closer to God. Today we should praise God, read scripture, be active in life, and get to know God personally by communicating eagerly with him daily. If we pray, we will be ready and willing to learn and to change into more perfect beings.

But grow in the grace and knowledge of our Lord and Savior Jesus Christ. To him be glory both now and forever! Amen. 2 Peter 3:18

Do your best to present yourself to God as one approved, a workman who does not need to be ashamed and who correctly handles the word of truth. 2 Timothy 2:15

For this very reason, make every effort to add to your faith goodness; and to goodness, knowledge; and to knowledge, self-control; and to self-control, perseverance; and to perseverance, godliness; and to godliness, brotherly kindness; and to brotherly kindness, love. For if you possess these qualities in increasing measure, they will keep you from being ineffective and unproductive in your knowledge of our Lord Jesus Christ. 2 Peter 1:5–8

And we, who with unveiled faces all reflect the Lord's glory, are being transformed into his likeness with ever-increasing glory, which comes from the Lord, who is the Spirit. 2 Corinthians 3:18

Then we will no longer be infants, tossed back and forth by the waves, and blown here and there by every wind of teaching and by the cunning and craftiness of men in their deceitful scheming. Instead, speaking the truth in love, we will in all things grow up into him who is the Head, that is, Christ. Ephesians 4:14, 15

THOUGHTS

Things of importance
Happiness revisited
Open invitations to
Us, to others
Given freely
Hoping to give
Thanks and cheer
Separately or in groups

Money is not important. Times spent with friends and relatives are. Memories sustain us, encourage us, and energize our lives. Wonderful memories are created when we freely share our time and ourselves with those around us.

We need to cherish those times and situations which come our way. It may be that perfect Christmas present you gave someone. It could be the wonderful time you had by just "dropping in" on a friend. It might be that comfort you provided to a loved one during a time of trial. Sharing songs at a nursing home not only brought joy to their hearts but also provided you with a warm feeling deep inside. Those memories can always be relived when we need a lift or a smile.

Take time to think. Be idle for half a day, not planning anything or doing anything special. That alone time, that idleness, can lead to thoughts, which can lead to happy memories. It is not wasted but time well spent on ourselves, a time to renew, reminisce, and smile.

Make sure you take time to relive those memories. It is comforting and a necessity in a world that spends too much time being busy.

The fruit of righteousness will be peace; the effect of righteousness will be quietness and confidence forever. Isaiah 32:17

What's Missing?

Children looking for presents
Heaping plates of cookies
Reindeer, Santa and his sleigh
Icicles and snowmen, hot chocolate
Sending out cards
Traveling home
Mom, Dad, kids, relatives
Anxious parents and children
Singing carols

All of the items mentioned above are part of our Christmas celebrations. Children are anxiously waiting and looking for the presents Santa will bring them. Mom, Dad, and the relatives are frantically shopping and preparing for the big day. Songs are sung about white Christmases, snow and mistletoe, reindeer, Santa and his sleigh, and traveling home. Icicles are part of the season "up North," and palm trees and cactus are fixtures "down South." Cookies, chocolate, and other goodies are made or purchased to make sure everyone is in the Christmas mood. Lights are everywhere.

The only thing missing in all of this is Christ. Jesus is the reason for the season. Too often that concept is completely forgotten. The effort and the attention is on the presents and decorating and not on the birth of the Savior of the world. Without Jesus there would be no Christmas, no reason to celebrate. We would all be damned, having no future and no hope. Our lives would be fruitless and without meaning.

The emphasis should always be on the Christ-child, the one who would save the world by taking on the sins of the world, dying, and rising from the dead. Christ should be the epicenter of our celebration, the one we worship and adore. We should sing the songs of praise. We should seek out those less fortunate than us to give presents to or be presents to them. Our anxiousness should be because we are preparing for the coming of the Savior. Jesus should be in our thoughts and actions at all times. Prayer should be the centerpiece of our celebration.

Start this Christmas by putting Christ back into the celebration. Make his birth be the heart of everything you say or do. Make Advent a real preparation time to welcome the Savior. Lessen your stress by putting your efforts into what is important and not to what the world expects. You can blissfully enjoy the season because your attention is on Christ and not commercial trappings and outward appearances. *And we have seen and testify that the father has sent his son to be the Savior of the world. 1 John 4:14*

And Mary said: "My soul glorifies the Lord and my spirit rejoices in God my Savior, for he has been mindful of the humble state of his servant. From now on all generations will call me blessed, for the Mighty One has done great things for me—holy is his name. His mercy extends to those who fear him, from generation to generation. Luke 1:46–50

Therefore God exalted him to the highest place and gave him the name that is above every name, that at the name of Jesus every knee should bow, in heaven and on earth and under the earth, and every tongue confess that Jesus Christ is Lord, to the glory of God the Father. Philippians 2:9